ANCIENT COIN COLLECTING II

Numismatic Art of the Greek World

WAYNE G. SAYLES

© 1997 by

Wayne G. Sayles

All rights reserved. No portion of this publication may be reproduced or transmitted in any form or by any means, electronic or mechanical, including photocopy, recording, or any information storage and retrieval system, without permission in writing from the publisher, except by a reviewer who may quote brief passages in a critical article or review to be printed in a magazine or newspaper, or electronically transmitted on radio or television.

Published by

700 E. State Street • Iola, WI 54990-0001
Telephone: 715/445-2214

Please call or write for our free catalog.
Our toll-free number to place an order or obtain a free catalog is 800-258-0929
or please use our regular business telephone 715-445-2214
for editorial comment and further information.

Library of Congress Catalog Number: 95-82428
ISBN: 0-87341-500-0

Printed in the United States of America

This book is dedicated to the memory of Warren G. Moon
late Professor of Art History
University of Wisconsin
who shared with this student his love of Greek art
and whose patience helped to bring
the sometimes bewildering subject into perspective.

PREFACE

This is the second volume of a series intended to introduce the broad field of ancient coinage to prospective new collectors. The first volume, *Ancient Coin Collecting*, was a road map to the hobby in a very general sense. The present volume focuses on one of the major categories of ancient coinage, that of the Greeks.

The organization of material in this volume is similar to that of its predecessor in that many short chapters deal with a variety of subjects. The intention of this approach is to increase the utility of the work as a desktop reference and locator. This book is a survey, and a brief one at that. It is not possible to examine the entire field of Greek coinage in a work of this size. The British Museum *Catalogue of Greek Coins* is comprised of 29 substantial volumes, and still, it is not comprehensive. Hopefully, this book will serve as a more detailed road map to the collecting of these particular coins, and will save the collector time and effort by synthesizing and distilling much of the information that every serious collector should learn.

Like its forerunner, this volume foregoes footnoting in favor of textual and bibliographic references. As an introductory work, we feel that the beginning collector will find this approach more "user-friendly" than the traditional approach required of scholarly writers. Where additional sources of information are recommended, we have provided a bibliography at the end of a section. These bibliographies are keyed to a chapter or section by the nature of the heading bar, which will match the appropriate text header—that is, it will be solid, screened or blank within the borders. We have attempted to render Greek place-names in the currently accepted method, but certain Latinized spellings have been retained due to their familiarity. Rendering well known names like Cleopatra as Kleopatra, Metapontum as Metapontion or Croesus as Kroisos seems unnecessarily pedantic.

Greek coins reflect the work of some of the greatest artists the world has known. Even tiny fractional denominations often bear images that are exceptional in design and execution. Although important to the study of history, geography and economics, they are more often recognized as extraordinary works of art—and are frequently collected as such, aside from their geopolitical aspects. As the title suggests, this book approaches ancient Greek numismatics from that perspective. Notwithstanding individual virtuosity, no other series of ancient coinage surpasses or even comes close to equalling in beauty the masterpieces of Greek numismatic art. Any novice collector can distinguish the difference between an archaic coin and one from the Hellenistic period. Being able to explain the difference is another matter. Understanding how the changes came to pass is still another matter. We hope that this becomes more apparent after consideration of the material presented here.

The study of Greek coins can require a lifetime of effort. It is not possible, even for the most astute collector, to learn all that there is to know about the field. The successful collector will learn to focus his or her attention on a succinct area which can be digested, understood, and mastered. This sort of specialization is exemplified by Dr. Brian Kritt's recent study, *Seleucid Coins of Bactria*. These coins represent a very tiny fraction of the coinage of the Greek world, but they are coins of interest to Dr. Kritt, who, as a professional numismatist, is also well versed in many other fields. Because of his personal interest in this limited, and relatively understudied field, Kritt was able to effectively analyze and completely reattribute the series to a new mint—helping to rewrite the history of Seleukid Baktria from a numismatic perspective. There are many areas of Greek numismatics where this is still possible, and exciting challenges await the intrepid and dedicated collector of Greek coins. Hopefully, the following chapters will provide an impetus for recognition, analysis, research and publication of similar new discoveries.

The illustrations in this text are intended to expose the reader to the beauty of Greek numismatic art. It is not likely that the average collector will ever own some of the coins depicted, but that should not be discouraging. There are many beautiful coins in this series that are easy to obtain at modest prices. It is our intention throughout to project visual images rather than to document specific coin types or specimens. Therefore, the illustrations herein are not necessarily presented at precisely the actual size. Where size varies significantly from the actual specimen, we have normally included a multiplier in parentheses.

Welcome to the wonderful world of ancient Greek coins!

Gainesville, Missouri 1997   W.G.S.

ACKNOWLEDGMENTS

We are indebted in particular to the late Professor Warren G. Moon, of the University of Wisconsin, who took us under his wing and guided our studies at that institution. As often is the case—even though we became close personal friends— the author did not truly appreciate the value of that association until some years later. Warren was an avid numismatist, and often used coin illustrations in his lectures to emphasize various styles or artistic conventions. He possessed a special talent for making ancient art and history come alive.

The works of Charles Seltman were inspirational as well. *An Approach to Greek Art*, provided our first encounter with the term "Celator", and engendered the transformation of an avocation into a career.

Illustrated in this volume are some of the finest Greek coins to have come on the ancient coin market in this century. We are deeply indebted to Leu Numismatik of Zürich, Switzerland for permission to illustrate coins sold by that firm at public auction. A great many of the rarities illustrated herein are reproduced from that source. Classical Numismatic Group, of Lancaster, Pennsylvania also provided many illustrations of exceptional coins sold by that firm. Harlan J. Berk, of Chicago, Illinois allowed reproduction of the wonderful Amphipolis tetradrachm illustrated in the "Masterpieces" section. We are also indebted to Harald Salvesen of Norway for permission to reproduce photos of the exceptional Athenian didrachm and tetradrachm of Orophernes in his collection, as well as the silver tetradrachms of Mithradates IV, Mithradates IV and Laodike, Ariarathes IV, Ariarathes V and Prusias II. Mr. William F. Spengler and Mr. Hakim Hamidi graciously provided illustrations of very rare Baktrian portrait coins from their personal files. The superb portrait of Eukratides was provided by Edward J. Waddell, and the first "wrestlers" coin and the "hoplite race" electrum hecte are from the collection of Anthony Milavic. We have borrowed illustrations of a few rare Baktrian coins from earlier published works of Newell, Whitehead and Gardner. Several other photos of rare Baktrian coins are by Andrew Daneman. Tradart of Geneva provided the Athenian tetradrachm illustration on our dust jacket. Line art illustrations were extracted from Duruy's *History of Greece*, 1890 edition. Dennis Kroh's *Ancient Coin Reference Reviews* were extremely helpful in compiling the bibliographies.

Dr. Alan Walker was kind enough to review parts of this volume, and offer very useful suggestions in advance of publication. His consideration and effort, on very short notice, is deeply appreciated.

As with Volume I, the assistance and constant encouragement of Doris J. Tobalske was invaluable. In addition to proofing manuscripts, and offering ideas from a fresh perspective, she assumed the burden of myriad tasks that would otherwise have gone unattended.

Contents

Voices from the Past 1
The Origin and Use of Coinage in the West 3
    ...... Bibliography: The Origin and Use of Coinage in the West 5
Production and Control 6
    ...... Bibliography: Production and Control 9
    Denominations 10
    Dating Greek Coins 13
    ...... Bibliography: Denominations / Dating 17
The World of the Greeks 18
    ...... Map: The World of the Greeks 18
    ...... Bibliography: The World of the Greeks 20
    Western Mediterranean 21
    ...... Mint Cities of Spain 21
    Magna Graecia / Italy 22
    ...... Bibliography: Magna Graecia / Italy 23
    ...... Mint Cities of Italy 24
    Sicily 25
    ...... Map: Sicily 25
    ...... Bibliography: Sicily 28
    ...... Mint Cities of Sicily 28
    Northern Greece / Thrace 29
    ...... The Macedonian Kingdom 31
    ...... The World of Alexander 33
    ......   Bibliography: Northern Greece / Thrace 35
    ......   Mint Cities of Northern Greece 35
    Western/Central Greece 36
    ...... Map: Western / Central Greece 36
    ...... League Coinage 38
    ......   Bibliography: League Coinage 40
    ...... Athens 41
    ......   Bibliography: Athens 43
    ...... Aigina 44
    ......   Bibliography: Aigina 44
    ......   Mint Cities of Western / Central Greece 45
    Peloponnesos 46
    ...... Map: Peloponnesos 46
    ...... Bibliography: Peloponnesos 48
    ...... Mint Cities of the Peloponnesos 48

Island Greeks 49
......Crete 52
......Cyprus 53
...... Map: Cyprus 53
...... Mint Cities of Island Greeks 54
...... Mint Cities of Crete 55
...... Mint Cities of Cyprus 55
......Bibliography: Island Greeks 55
Black Sea Area 56
......Bibliography: Black Sea Area 58
......Mint Cities of the Black Sea 58
......The Black Sea "Hoard" 59
......Map: The Black Sea 59
Asia Minor 60
......Stephanophoroi of Aiolis and Ionia 62
......Bibliography: Asia Minor 65
......Mint Cities of Asia Minor 66
The East 69
......Map: The East 69
......Phoenicia 70
......Bibliography: The East 71
......Mint Cities of The East 71
North Africa 72
......Mint Cities of North Africa 73
......Map: North Africa 73
Artistry of the Celator 74
......Bibliography: Artistry of the Celator 79
Celators who signed their works 80
......Bibliography: Celators who signed their works 85
Symbolism in Greek Art 86
Canting Puns 89
Optical Trickery 90
Senescence in Numismatic Art 91
Greek Dress and Hair Styles 92
......Bibliography: Greek Dress and Hair Styles 93
Mythology and Coin Motifs 94
......Herakles and the Nemean Lion 95
......The Rape of Kassandra 98
......Oedipus and the Sphinx 100
......Theseus and the Minotaur 102
......Europa and the Bull 103
......Bibliography: Mythology and Coin Motifs 104
Athletes and Athletic Events 105
......Bibliography: Athletes and Athletic Events 108

The Periods of Greek Art 109
...... Bibliography: The Periods of Greek Art 110
The Archaic Period 111
...... Incuse designs on Archaic Greek coins 114
...... Bibliography: The Archaic Period 116
The Classical Period 117
The Hellenistic Period 119
...... Hellenistic Portraiture 120
......   Bibliography: Hellenistic Portraiture 120
......   Alexander the Great 124
......   Kings of Northern Greece and Asia Minor 125
......   The Seleukid Dynasty 135
......   Bibliography: The Seleukid Dynasty 142
......   The Ptolemaic Dynasty 143
......   The Bactrian Kings 147
......   Family of Hieron II 157

Masterpieces of Greek Art 158

Appendix I: Glossary 186
Appendix II: Table of Events 188
Appendix III: Additional References 189
Appendix IV: General Index 190

Voices from the Past

History is the recorded experience of man, but all historical accounts are influenced to some degree by the perceptions and prejudices of the recorder. While it is exciting to examine events through the comments of ancient writers, we should remember that the authors of surviving works from antiquity often were removed in time and circumstance from the subjects that they wrote about. Modern readers who rely faithfully and uncritically on accounts from Greek and Latin literature may come to conclusions which are inaccurate. Nevertheless, literature is an enlightening source of information.

Homer

Ancient writers have left a wealth of information, and much of it survived in spite of the ravages of time. Some of it is quite useful to the numismatist in understanding the designs on coins. Strabo's *Geography*, written during the reign of Augustus, is one of the most important works surviving from antiquity. Pliny the Elder wrote a lengthy treatise in the mid-first century AD on the nature of practically everything in the universe known to the Romans. One surviving chapter of his *Natural History* is dedicated to art. This account includes an invaluable listing of sculptors (mainly Greek) and their works. Some of Pliny's comments shed light on the role that art played in contemporary society—at least in the lives of educated Romans. A century later, Pausanius recorded the sculpture that was still standing or that was still remembered by local citizens in his *Guide to Greece*. Many of the monumental works mentioned by Pausanius appear as images on Greek and Roman coinage of cities at or near the various sites. Two important numismatists of the late 19th century, Percy Gardner and Friederich Imhoof-Blumer, did an analysis of the works described by Pausanius which appear on coins. Their article for the *Journal of Hellenic Studies* (1885-1887) was reprinted under a new title in 1964. Although somewhat dated, *Ancient Coins Illustrating Lost Masterpieces of Greek Art, a Numismatic Commentary on Pausanius* is still very educational and entertaining.

Although the direct mention of coins in ancient writings is infrequent, many of the references to sculpture and to collecting are useful to modern numismatists. Another work of the past century which is still useful to those who study and collect coins as works of art is *Select Passages From Ancient Writers Illustrative Of The History Of Greek Sculpture* by H. Stuart Jones. The 1966 reprint of this work, published by Argonaut, contains a very thorough and helpful index. Dictionaries of Classical Biography, Geography, Mythology, etc. were produced in some profusion toward the end of the 19th century. They can be very useful, but information should always be verified by more current sources if possible—much has been learned about the ancient world in the past 100 years! There are several modern compilations of extracts from ancient texts which are also useful to the numismatist. Two of particular merit are J.J. Pollitt's *The Art of Greece, 1400-31 B.C.* (Prentice-Hall Sources and Documents series), and Stephen Miller's *Arete, Greek Sports From Ancient Sources* (University of California Press).

Coins are a visual record of man's experiences. Although a less narrative form of history than literature, the story that they tell often may be extracted through careful analysis. Aside from the information in its legends and iconography, a coin may reveal much about the time and place of its issue. Chronology is one of the aspects of history which has benefited greatly from numismatic research. Coins do not have faulty memories or confuse one personage with another. They relate to us the same information that they related to someone living at the time of their issue. It is our task to correctly interpret that information and place it in its proper context.

There are a number of things about a coin's design, or its production, that may shed light on contemporary history. Not all of them are readily apparent. There are certain coins that are like chronological mileposts. Because of the particular circumstances associated with their issue, we can date them precisely. The dating of related coins can often be interpolated from these mileposts through die-links, over-strikes, and stylistic similarities. This form of numismatic analysis is generally dependable because the coins speak for themselves.

Where we run into trouble as numismatists is when we try to guess at the meaning of an image or link the issue of a coin to some specific event based on circumstantial evidence. Occasionally this can be done with confidence, but more often we find ourselves wading through a quagmire of conjecture before we eventually find the truth. Still, it is this conjecture that spurs thought, and new hypotheses that spark rebuttal. Through the process of challenge we are able to test theories that lead ultimately to consensus and better understanding of the ancient world. A classic example of this may be seen in dating the reigns of historically obscure rulers. Ancient writers were notoriously bad with dates, and in most cases cannot be trusted without alternative confirmation. The Baktrian series is fraught with problems when it comes to dating. The recent work of O. Bopearachchi has moved us in the right direction, but there still are many uncertainties.

Numismatic research is like a complex puzzle. It is our challenge to try to understand the past sufficiently to place a coin in its proper context, and to extract from it all of the information that it can provide about its time and place of origin. That is the joy of ancient numismatics. The more involved one becomes, the clearer we can hear those voices from the past.

The Origin and Use of Coinage in the West

Most scholars of the 19th and early 20th centuries placed the invention of coinage in Lydia at about 700 BC. In this century, there has been much debate over the issue and the result has been a reappraisal which places the event nearer the end of the seventh century. How, with any certainty, can we place a date on an event which has gone unrecorded? The coins themselves are not dated in any way.

In 1904, British excavations at the Temple of Artemis at Ephesos unearthed a deposit of about 90 electrum coins. Some were unmarked lumps of electrum of uniform weight, others were typeless and marked with a simple punch, others bore a combination of animal representations and punch marks. The analysis and interpretation of this find has been at the heart of the dating issue. These coins were originally determined to be from an earlier strata than the Temple of Artemis founded during the reign of King Croesus (acceded in 560 BC), therefore, they logically should be dated to an earlier reign. Ash in the excavation was seen as residue from the destruction of a temple in 652, during a Cimmerian invasion. Seltman suggested *(Greek Coins)* that the coins were from an earlier time. If this was the case, the earliest of the electrum coins could be dated to the reign of Gyges (685-652 BC) or earlier.

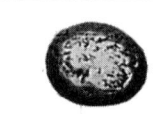
Lydia, "typeless" EL 1/3 stater ca. 620 BC or earlier

Lydia, EL 1/3 stater end of the 7th century

Ionia, EL stater, before 560 BC

Gyges was the founder of the Mermnad Dynasty, which adopted as its royal arms the image of the lion. This symbol appears on the coinage of Lydia, through the reign of Croesus, in several varieties. The chronology of these lion figured coins is aided by the addition on certain specimens of the name WALWET in Lydian script—interpreted as "Alyattes" in Greek. Alyattes, the father of Croesus, ruled ca. 615-560. Ironically, the Greeks referred to the Lydians as "Barbarians". Their language, being strange to the Greek ear sounded like the *bar bar* of sheep. This term was applied to all non-Greek speaking people. In modern times we consider their coinage as part of the Greek world.

Very recent scholarship and debate has cast doubt on the whole issue of the temple destruction, extent of the Cimmerian invasion, and dating of the electrum coins. There may not have been an earlier temple, and ash at the site could have come from foundation ceremonies. Dates will probably be readjusted once more, and one should not rely too strongly on any published dates at this point.

If the Lydians were indeed the first to sanction an official coinage—and this is far from certain—their lead was quickly followed. Ionian electrum coins have also been dated, with relative certainty, to the same period as the Artemision deposit. By the middle of the sixth century there were probably a half dozen or more mints in operation. With the proliferation of issuing authorities came a growing need for identifiable symbols to distinguish one from another. Often, the images selected for the earliest issues of a city-state were retained through centuries of minting activity. This would suggest that those images were deeply rooted in the culture of the locale where they appeared.

Coins were struck primarily in four metals: gold, electrum (an alloy of gold and at least 20% silver), silver and bronze (an alloy of copper and tin). Issues in any other metals are very rare—although there were a few in nickel or billon. The ancients understood how to purify metals, and were surprisingly successful in maintaining close tolerances. One early development was the division of value by metal and weight—which we know as denominations. There are identifiable denominations among some of the earliest electrum coins, including those without images, and during the reign of Croesus (560-546 BC) a system using pure gold and silver coins was instituted.

The introduction of bronze coins during the fifth century added a new dimension to the use of coins as a monetary instrument. With a series of denominations ranging to the tiniest fraction of a gold stater, it became possible for the average person in the street to use coins for transacting business of almost any nature from buying a loaf of bread to paying for services, entertainment, transportation and, of course, taxes. The first bronze coins appeared in Sicily and at about the same time in the Black Sea area. By the first half of the fourth century they were struck at mints throughout the Mediterranean.

One question that always seems to spark the interest of collectors is "What could one buy with a drachm or tetradrachm at the time of its issue?" From our own experience, we know that a top-of-the-line new automobile in 1960 cost about $3,000. That same automobile in 1997 will cost over $30,000. On the other hand, a portable color TV in 1960 would have cost about $300, while the same set in 1997 would sell for less than $100. Over that 36-year period the dollar bill has not changed in appearance, but its purchasing power is quite different, for many reasons. The ancients endured similar experiences with inflation and supply. The point, simply, is that comparisons are risky. The best that we can do is try to measure the costs of goods against income at any given point in history. Fortunately, classical literature is full of references to the cost of things. Below is a chart of incomes and expenses in the fifth to fourth centuries BC. Keep in mind that all of these price comparisons are unreliable without careful analysis of conditions at the point of reference. Nevertheless it is interesting to see the comparative value of goods then as opposed to now.

Daily Income	Expenses
Acropolis laborer ..... 1 drachm *Architect .... 2 drachms* *Ceramic potter .... 1 drachm* *Hoplite at siege ...... 2 drachms* *Housemaid .... 2 obols* *Mud carrier .... 3 obols* *Navy technician .... 1 drachm* *Seasonal laborer .... 2 obols* *Slave miner (+ food) ..... 1 obol* *Temple builder ..... 2.5 drachms*	*Athens' walls .... 17 million dr.* *Axe .... 2 drachms* *Cow .... 50 drachms* *Figs, dried, 25 Kilo ... 1 drachm* *Goat .... 10 drachms* *Horse .... 1,200 drachms* *House .... 2,000 drachms* *Olive oil, 1 liter .... 3 obols* *Salt fish, 1 piece .... 2 obols* *Shoes .... 8 drachms* *Trireme .... 6,000 drachms* *Wheat, 25 Kilo .... 3 drachms* *Wine, 5 liters .... 1 drachm*

BIBLIOGRAPHY
The Origin and Use of Coinage in the West

Babelon, Ernest. *Traité des monnais greques et romaines"*, 1901-1932, Forni reprint 1976.

Cole, T.J. "The Lifetime of Coins in Circulation", *Numismatic Chronicle*, 1976.

Daehn, William E. "Evidence for the invention of coinage: Artemision hoard launches debate", *The Celator*, Vol. 6, No. 1, Jan. 1992.

Howgego, C.J. "Why did ancient states strike coins?", *Numismatic Chronicle*, 1990.

MacDonald, G. *Coin Types, Their Origin and Development*, Glasgow, 1905.

Robinson, E.S.G. "The Coins from the Ephesian Artemision Reconsidered", *Journal of Hellenic Studies* LXXI, 1951.

_____. "The date of the earliest coins", *Numismatic Chronicle*, 1956.

Vickers, Michael. "Early Greek Coinage, a Reassessment", *Numismatic Chronicle*, 1985.

Waddingham, Gary. "Literary sources reveal buying power of the drachm", *The Celator*, Vol. 2, No. 5, May 1988.

Production and Control

The production of coinage requires not only technical skill, but the availability of precious and semiprecious metals. A small city or minor kingdom might be able to obtain sufficient material through trade to produce coinage for its own needs, but a major economic or political power needed access to large quantities of gold and silver. The ability of a power to satisfy this need often determined its success or failure. Among the great powers of the Classical and Hellenistic periods we find that most had access to important mines. Athens, for example, drew tremendous wealth from the Laurion silver mines, while Aigina derived its silver from the mines on Siphnos. Philip II was able to finance his military exploits with silver from Damastion and Paeonia while his son Alexander inherited fortunes in gold and silver from conquests in Asia. The Ptolemaic dynasty enjoyed a supply of gold from the mines in Nubia and copper from their mines in Cyprus. The Seleukids drew their wealth from sources in Asia Minor and the eastern provinces conquered by Alexander. John Hiller compiled an excellent overview of gold mining and the use of gold in antiquity for *The Celator* (see map on following page).

Converting raw metal into coinage was a technical feat of some wonderment. Each coin was individually struck, by hand, on a carefully prepared planchet which was cast in a mold of fire clay at exactly

Miners at work:— from a plaque discovered at Corinth

the right weight. Heating it to precisely the right temperature, a mint worker struck the planchet between hardened dies with just enough force to transfer an image squarely onto the coin's surface. This process is all the more remarkable when we consider that it must have been repeated thousands of times in a day. In certain issues we see a conscious attempt to align the images (die axis) on a coin's obverse and reverse. This could be assured by hinging the two dies, but Greek coins were generally produced from unhinged dies. An alignment mark on the dies may have served the same purpose, as similarities in orientation sometimes suggest.

Dies were generally carved in bronze, brass or iron which could be worked while still soft and then hardened for striking. Any given issue of coinage for a major city or kingdom might number in the hundreds of thousands or even in the millions. Obviously, this required a well organized and intensive effort. Because the life expectancy of a die was rather short (estimates range between 10,000 and 30,000 coins), most coin types are represented by a substantial number of dies. As dies fractured during production they were often sent back to the celator for recutting. There are also known cases of dies from one ruler being recut to use for coinage of a successor. This would seem to imply that, at least in Greek times, die engraving was a time consuming and expensive element of production.

The elements of design were usually integrated with the technical needs of production. That is, the point of highest relief was intention-

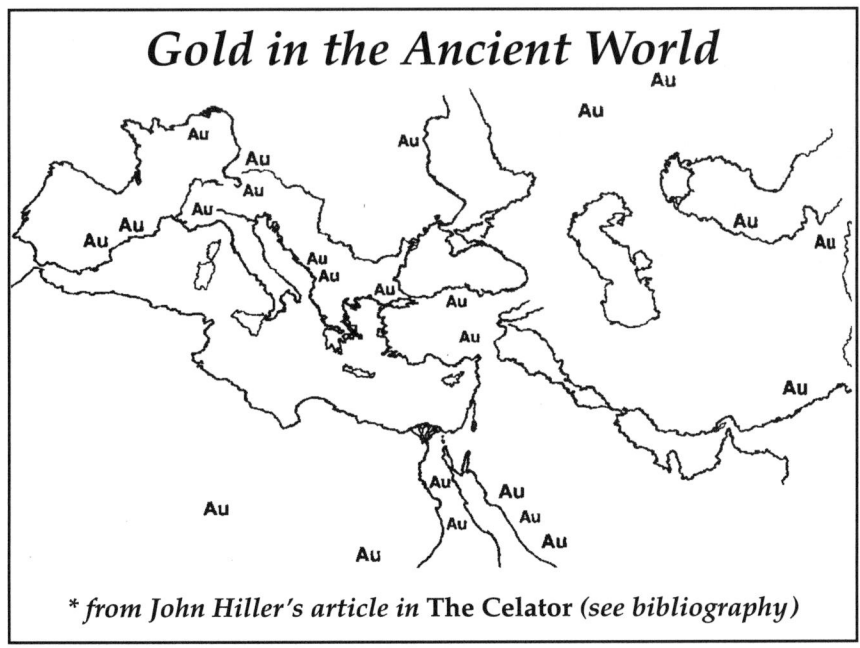

from John Hiller's article in **The Celator** *(see bibliography)*

ally placed at the center of the obverse die so that the stress from striking would flow outward from that point. The obverse die was set into an anvil and was the lower of the two. In many cases, dies were intentionally carved with a slight "set" to them. In other words, the plane upon which the image was engraved was not absolutely flat—the obverse die having a slight concavity and the reverse die a corresponding convexity. This reduced slippage between the die and planchet. Therefore, Greek coins often are slightly concave on the reverse and convex on the obverse. Slippage was also reduced through the incorporation of a circular border of line, dots or a more intricate pattern around the periphery of the die. Since the Greeks did not use a collar to contain the struck metal, the shape of each coin varies. Sometimes the shape is quite unusual and can either complement or interfere with the design. The tools of the celator's trade were similar to those used for the carving of gemstones. While coins were a relatively late innovation, the engraving of seals and signets was a very well established trade. Sumerian and other Near Eastern stones bear engravings from as early as the fourth millennium BC. The celator's tools included gravures, burrs, bow-drills, chisels and almost certainly the use of magnifying devices (see bibliography).

Naturally, the exchange of any material or service for coinage requires some control of the coinage itself in terms of value and acceptability. With precious metals, weight was a logical measure. There were no International Monetary Commissions to set standards or fix rates of exchange. Standards were, nevertheless, adopted independently by a number of the more important commercial centers. The Corinthian drachm, for example, was struck on a standard of 2.85 grams. The Athenian drachm was struck at a weight of just over 4 grams, and the drachm at Aigina weighed in at over 6 grams. The Rhodian drachm weighed about 3.5 grams. Even with these differences in weight standards, as long as each issuing authority maintained strict control of weights and purity, daily trade did not require the weighing of each individual coin. The placement of stamps, badges or names on coins helped to serve as a guarantee of this quality control.

It was inevitable that certain individuals and even some political regimes would attempt to issue or exchange coinage with less intrinsic value than its accepted face value. One method of cheating on the content was the plating of a copper core which we refer to as "fourré." It is debatable whether official mints engaged in the production of fourrés, setting aside the case of Athens and its emergency coinage of 406. The fact that they were a widespread problem in certain periods is attested by the number of surviving coins with test cuts and "banker's marks".

Countermarking of coins by mint authorities was perhaps not as common in Greek issues as it later became under the Roman administration of those lands, but it was nonetheless an accepted practice. Indeed, certain coins are more commonly found with countermarks than without. The main reasons for countermarking were to authorize certain coins for payment of public debts or to retariff coins for acceptance at a different value. Coins struck at special events, like the games at Olympia, were sometimes countermarked to signify their validity for continued use. Coins of an earlier reign could be revalidated by applying a countermark which would save the expense of reminting.

Sinope, AR didrachm, ca. 290-250 BC Helios / Poseidon countermark

Counce­marks are not often thought of as artistic, but in the Greek series, a countermark can be a thing of beauty. A third century silver didrachm from Sinope in Paphlagonia was countermarked with a magnificent two sided stamp. The heads of Helios and Poseidon on the countermark illustrated above are as well executed as any from contemporary dies for a regular coin issue. Within the rays of the facing Helios are tiny letters which read ΣΙΝΩΠΕΩΝ!

BIBLIOGRAPHY
Production and Control

Burford, Alison. *Craftsmen in Greek and Roman Society.* Cornell, 1972.
Cooper, Denis R. *The Art and Craft of Coinmaking: A History of Minting Technology,* London 1988.
Esty, Warren W. "Estimating the size of a coinage", *Numismatic Chronicle,* 1984.
Hill, G.F. "Ancient Methods of Coining", *Numismatic Chronicle,* 1922.
Hiller, John. "The beginnings of coinage were prompted by the evolution of the use and value of gold", *The Celator,* Vol. 5, No. 8. August 1991
Roebuck, Carl. *The Muses at Work,* MIT Press, 1969.
Seibert, Robert. "Literary sources and historical records indicate optical aid", *The Celator,* Vol. 4, No. 4, (April, 1990).
Sellwood, D.G. "Some experiments in Greek minting technique", *Numismatic Chronicle,* 1963.
Tameanko, M. "Literature Points Out Knowledge of Magnifiers", *The Celator,* Vol 3, No. 6, (June, 1989).

Denominations

Determining the denomination (unit of value) of a Greek coin can be one of the most perplexing challenges facing a new collector. There are not only a plethora of denominations to deal with, but also a bewildering number of weight standards, modified standards, reduced standards, etc. Needless to say, there have been many theories advanced in this regard. While the whole issue of weight standards seems very complex from our perspective, it would have been much easier for merchants in a narrow window of the ancient world to understand and deal with the variances.

The following charts provide some standard weights and major denominations from a few of the more important minting authorities. These standards tend to vary slightly with time and circumstance, so don't panic if your tetradrachm seems a little too light or too heavy. The Athe-

Table of Greek Weight Standards

Standard	Major Unit	Weight
Achaean	stater (3 drachms)	8.0 gm
Aiginetan	stater (2 drachms)	12.2 gm
Asiatic	tetradrachm	13.3 gm
Attic	tetradrachm	17.2 gm
Campanian	stater (2 drachms)	7.5 gm
Chian	tetradrachm	15.6 gm
Cistophoric	tetradrachm	12.6 gm
Corcyrean	stater (2 drachms)	11.6 gm
Corinthian	stater (3 drachms)	8.6 gm
Euboic	stater (2 drachms)	17.2 gm
Lycian	stater (2 drachms)	8.6 / 10 gm
Persian	siglos	8.35 / 8.55 gm
Phoenician	shekel (2 drachms)	7.0 gm
Ptolemaic	tetradrachm	14.3 gm
Rhodian	tetradrachm	13.2 / 15.2 gm
Sicilian	litra	.86 gm

For a very useful discussion of weight standards we recommend the article *"Making sense of Greek coin weight standards"* by William E. Daehn (see bibliography).

nian tetradrachm, for example, fell in weight from over 17 grams to under 15 grams during the third and second centuries. Weights of individual coins are sometimes greatly affected by damage or conditions of preservation and may fall short of the standard. Although weight is often considered a test of authenticity, it is only one consideration and must be taken in context with other pertinent factors.

Gold Denominations

The list below gives a relational comparison of gold (AV) denominations based on the Stater as a standard unit. It is arranged sequentially from the lowest in value to highest. The numbers in parentheses represent the number of a listed unit equalling one stater, or the number of staters in a listed unit. Electrum (EL) is an alloy of gold and at least 20% silver.

El twelfth (12)
El Hektai (6)
El third (3)
EL STATER

AV Hemiobol (24)
AV Obol (12)
AV Diobol (4)
AV Tetrobol / Hemistater (2)
AV Octobol / STATER
AV Octadrachm

Silver Denominations

This list gives a relational comparison of silver denominations based on the drachm as a standard unit. The number in parentheses represents the number of listed units in a drachm or the number of drachms in the listed unit. There are exceptions to this simplified comparison. For example, the Corinthian Stater is divided into three drachms rather than two, and the Sicilian litra (.86 gm) stands alone with larger denominations being measured as multiples.

Hemiobol (12)
Tritartemorion (9)
Obol (6)
Trihemiobol (4)
Diobol (3)
Hemidrachm/Triobol (2)
Tetrobol (1.5)
DRACHM

DRACHM
Didrachm/Stater/Nomos (2)
Tetradrachm (4)
Octadrachm (8)
Dekadrachm (10)
Dodekadrachm (12)

Bronze Denominations

The list below gives a relational comparison of bronze denominations based on the Sicilian Onkia as a standard unit. Like the previous two charts, it is arranged sequentially from the lowest in value to highest. The numbers in parentheses represent the number of onkia in a listed unit. This standard was eventually adopted by most Sicilian cities, and some bronzes of this system bear marks of value. Bronze coins of other Greek cities and regions are generally categorized by diameter in millimeters since the actual denominations are usually unknown.

        ONKIA .... (1)
        Hexas .... (2)
        Trias .... (3)
        Tetras .... (4)
        Pentonkion .... (5)
        Hemilitron .... (6)
        Dekonkion .... (10)
        Litra* .... (12)

* The litra appears both as a silver and a bronze denomination, and is roughly equivalent to 1.2 silver obols of the mainland Greek cities. The bronzes from Athens classified as chalkoi are similar to the above in the sense that they are subdivisions (1/8th) of a silver obol. The dichalkon, a frequently encountered denomination, is therefore equivalent to 1/4 obol.

Another subject, related to standards, is the relationship between metals. Bronze was, in virtually all cases a token coinage and its intrinsic value bore no relationship to its value as legal tender. During the monetary crisis of 406, Athens issued bronze coins at the value of silver. When financial conditions improved, bronze was demonetized abruptly in 393—much to the chagrin of some merchants, as Aristophanes relates in his contemporary comedy "The Ecclesiazusae." The first standard to deal with this bimetallic relationship was that imposed by King Croesus of Lydia. Under his system the value ratio of silver to gold was 13.3 to 1. The ratio at Aigina, according to Ridgeway and acknowledged by Head, was 15:1, but this is still argued. Seltman relates silver to iron at Aigina with a ratio of 400:1. The arguments are endless and extremely difficult to follow.

Dating Greek Coins

The dating of Greek coins can present an interesting challenge to numismatists. Anepigraphic coins, those without inscriptions, may require a great deal of detective work to place into their proper chronology. Others, bearing names, monograms or symbols may be less enigmatic. Many coins struck during the Hellenistic Period actually bear dates. In these cases, it is possible to determine much about economic and/or political conditions or events of a specific time.

The Greeks did not follow a universal dating system like we do in our time, that was a much later invention. They did, however, possess an appreciation of history and they recognized the value of recording important events. The ancients measured time in several ways. The most common systems found on coins recorded regnal years or era years. (In some cases even the part of a year or the month of issue was recorded—as at Athens with its unique numbering system. Regnal dating began with the accession of a ruler, and started over when a new ruler came to power. The Ptolemies of Egypt used such a system. Era dates were generally tied to the founding year of a city or dynasty.

In both cases, the dates are typically recorded as letters of the Greek alphabet. The year 1, for example, appears as A (alpha), the year 2 as B (beta), and so on. Sometimes the numbers became quite high and letters representing 10s and 100s were added to the unit designator. In contrast to our modern convention, they normally were recorded (left to right) with the unit first, then the 10s digit and finally the 100s digit. Thusly, the year 123 was written ΓΚΡ (3+20+100). It is not unknown, however, for dates to be recorded in the opposite direction, i.e. 123 as ΡΚΓ. This seldom causes confusion since the resulting number often becomes nonsensical when read "backwards".

There were a number of major events in ancient history from which era dates were derived. Since

GREEK DATES

1	A	20	K	100	P
2	B	30	Λ	200	Σ
3	Γ	40	M	300	T
4	Δ	50	N	400	Y
5	E	60	Ξ	500	Φ
6	S	70	O	600	X
7	Z	80	Π	700	Ψ
8	H	90	ϙ	800	Ω
9	Θ				
10	I				

Greek dates are written in letters, and are read either from right to left or left to right. For example, the year 123 is written ΓΚΡ or ΡΚΓ, depending on the time and place. Since their calendar year did not start on January 1, as ours does, a Greek year will be expressed in overlapping dates like 148/7 BC or AD 147/8.

these dates were not of equal importance to everyone, we find that the era dates overlap. When interpreting the date recorded on a coin, it is critical to apply the proper dating era. It is also important not to confuse other control marks, like magistrate's initials, with dates. In at least one case, issues were numbered serially irrespective of date—no doubt to confuse collectors of a later era!

TYPICAL ERA DATES	
	from:
Seleukid Kingdom	312 BC
Kings of Pontos & Bithynia	297 BC
Arados, Phoenicia	259 BC
Tyre, Phoenicia	126 BC
Tripolis, Phoenicia	112 BC
Seleukeia, Syria	109 BC
Askalon, Judaea	104 BC
Mithradatic War	88 BC
Berytos	81 BC

Sometimes, when the motif is ambiguous, a date on the coin may help to form the basis of an attribution. In other cases, dated coins may provide the chronology of a magistrate's term or of a change in ruling authority. Dates coupled with changes in the weight or purity of an issue may pinpoint important internal changes, or an economic crises, and shed light on other related events. The usefulness of a date is obvious, and numismatic researchers are always thrilled to discover an unrecorded date among new finds. The bad news is that not enough coins are dated!

Magistrate's initials or monograms often appear in the fields of a coin design. These devices are also useful in establishing the chronology of a series, even when dates are absent. In a few cases, magistrates whose identifying marks appear on coins can be linked with individuals known through other historical records. Since magistrates were normally elected officials with a term of one year, a sequential arrangement of magistrates' names is essentially comparable to a dating system. Even when these magistrates are unknown to us historically, we can develop a fairly accurate chronology of their service by analyzing the coins bearing their marks.

Another historical occurrence that can help us to date a series of coins is the change of a place-name. As the result of conquest, or re-founding after some natural disaster, cities were often renamed. This sometimes happened two or three times over the "lifetime" of a city. When the historical record allows us to date these changes, it is easy enough to chronologically group the coins issued there by the name that they bear. Events of some importance, like victories at important games or battles, were often commemorated on coinage. Although we cannot precisely date coins based on the appearance of a commemorative motif, we can at least establish that they were issued no earlier than the date of the commemorated activity.

Because wear and die-breaks are progressive, we can determine the relative sequence of issue for certain coins. For illustration purposes, let's say that among the coins of a large hoard there are three different magistrates identifiable from reverse die symbols. We'll name them magistrate A, B and C. The coins belonging to magistrate A are uniformly worn, while those belonging to B and C are virtually unworn. This immediately suggests that magistrate A preceded B and C because his coins had been in circulation for some time before they were deposited. Among the coins belonging to magistrates B and C, we find one of each sharing a common obverse die. If the degree of obverse die wear can be determined, or a progressive flaw like a die-break can be found, we can thereby establish the relative chronology between the two magistrates.

Die links are a very useful phenomenon and occur as a result of the difference in the average life of obverse and reverse dies. Because they are imbedded in an anvil, obverse dies tend to outlast reverse (punch) dies by a factor of seven or eight to one. Therefore, we find that several reverse dies will be paired with the same obverse die. When the obverse die did eventually fail, it was not likely that the reverse die also needed immediate replacement. The reverse die in service at that time would have been used in conjunction with a new obverse die. This links two obverse dies in a determinable sequence. The direction of the sequence (first to last) can be ascertained by the state of wear exhibited on the obverse die at each pairing.

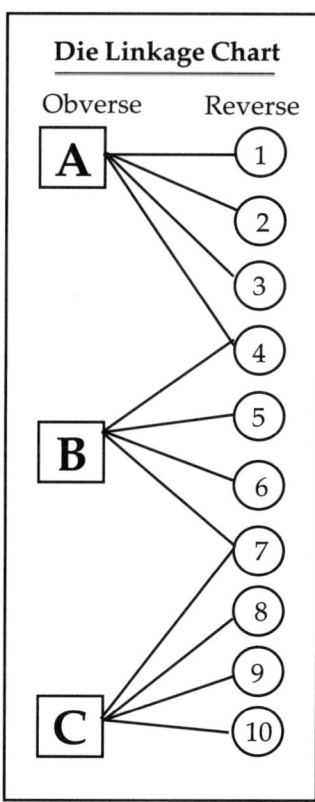

The accompanying chart graphically illustrates the nature of die linking. Coins A4 and B4 share a common reverse die, as do coins B7 and C7. Obverse die B will exhibit progressive wear as it is struck with reverse dies five through seven (perhaps 10,000 impressions each), so a deterioration of the die with each new pairing establishes the earliest and latest pairings in the sequence. The same is true of obverses A and C. The result is a sequence, that may determine a chronology.

Die studies have done more to advance our knowledge of the past than practically any other single research tool. Today, with improved imagery, collectors can compare a newly acquired specimen to those recorded in a growing number of reference works and sale catalogues. One advantage of this vast visual resource is that die studies can be performed on a series without physically examining every coin, or limiting research to hoard material. One of the many uses of a die study is to identify the origin of specimens that are otherwise unattributable. An obverse die-link to coins of a known mint may, for example, extend the corpus of reverse types for that mint, including the names or monograms of unrecorded magistrates, dates of issue, control symbols or thematic variations. The utility of this approach becomes obvious in a series like that of the Alexander type tetradrachms. Of course the size of an issue may be estimated from the number of dies extant, but this is hazardous speculation and should not be taken too seriously, a hoard may show up tomorrow with 20 new dies!

There are many other clues which help to establish relative chronology, and the corporate effort of numismatists over decades and even centuries has resulted in a tremendous amount of information about the production and control of coins at ancient mints. This sort of numismatic sleuthing is not relegated solely to museum curators and academics, it is also a worthy undertaking for collectors. There are so many coin types surviving from antiquity that the academic world is overwhelmed with material harboring potential discoveries.

The majority of Greek coins are not dated. In fact, many bear no inscriptions at all. Many others bear only the name or abbreviated letters representing the name of the issuing city. Dating these coins can be problematic. One accepted method of dating coins is by style and fabric. Among Greek coins, the three major classifications recognized today are derived from corresponding periods of artistic style. These periods, Archaic, Classical and Hellenistic are described in the following chapter. This method of classification and dating, while generally useful, requires some precaution. It was not unusual for artists of the Classical or Hellenistic periods to portray their subject in a manner common to an earlier age.

This convention is referred to as archaizing. For example, we normally equate incuse punches with coinage of the earliest period. Yet coins from the island of Aigina, and several other less important sites, used incuse punches or designs well into the Hellenistic Period. Likewise, features of earlier sculptural technique were often imitated by artists of a later

Tetradrachms of Patraos

Apollo — archaizing style

Apollo — classical style

period. One type of silver tetradrachm issued by King Patraos of Paeonia during the mid-fourth century portrays a laureate head of Apollo with the frontal "almond" eye common to art of a century earlier. Another contemporary tetradrachm of this ruler portrays the same Apollo with the "modern" profile eye typical at that time (see illustration on preceding page). The contrast is not one of stylistic transition, but rather of artistic intention. In fact, the archaizing version seems to have been issued toward the end of the series.

Many other examples of archaizing may be cited, and it is important to distinguish the archaic from the archaizing. Generally, the first indication of period is in the fabric of the planchet—which artists did not control. A typical third century planchet with an archaic style composition will seem unusual to a collector who has studied coins of the earlier era.

It is very difficult for an artist to work in a style that is not of his own time and experience. Inevitably, an attempt to copy work of an earlier age will result in something that does not quite "work". In other words, the feeling of the composition is artificial. This is exemplified by the archaizing tetradrachm of Patraos mentioned above. Although the eye is drafted in the frontal almond style of the Archaic Period, the portrait-like presentation of the subject is obviously Classical. In this case, any further doubt would be eliminated by looking at the reverse motif—a mounted warrior spearing a fallen enemy, which is entirely classical in style. Another example of an archaizing motif may be seen in the "Nike" of 420 BC from Caria (See under "Masterpieces of Greek Art").

BIBLIOGRAPHY
Denominations / Dating

Cope, Stephen N. "The Statistical Analysis of Coin Weights by Computer and a Rationalized Method for Producing Histograms", *Numismatic Chronicle*, 1980.

Daehn, William E. "Contradictory theories: Making sense of Greek coin weight standards", *The Celator*, Vol. 5, No. 8, August 1991.

Esty, Warren W. "Percentile Plots and Other Methods of Graphing Coin Weights", *Numismatic Chronicle*, 1989.

Ridgeway, William. *The Origin of Metallic Currency and Weight Standards*, Cambridge University Press, 1892.

Sear, David R. *Greek Coins and Their Values*, 2 vols., London, 1994.

Vagi, David L. "Weight standards important to monetary systems", *The Celator*, Vol. 8, No. 10, October 1994.

The World of the Greeks

With the exception of Alexander's brief excursions in the East, and the dynasty established by his successors in Baktria, the Greek world was primarily one which depended upon sea lanes for commerce and communication. The Greeks were a seafaring people from before the dawn of history, and the proliferation of their culture was due largely to the opportunities afforded them by the sea. They were not a coherent nation as we know the concept, but rather a heterogeneous collection of people with differing traditions and independent natures. Their world consisted mainly of the lands touching the Mediterranean and the Black Seas. From Athens, for example, relatively small craft could make their way to ports in the Bosporos, Spain, North Africa, Egypt and the trading meccas of Syria and Phoenicia.

Out of this grew standard trade routes, and great trading centers, which brought together myriad diverse cultures. Silphium from Kyrene, frankincense and myrrh from the land of Sheba, honey from Ephesos, and silks from the caravan traders drew merchant vessels from and to all parts of the Greek world. In exchange for these goods, payment was often demanded in precious metals. Consequently, a large number of coins were struck with the intended purpose of facilitating trade. These coins were, in a way, the first "trade dollars". They circulated over a wide geographical region, and were generally accepted in trade at places far removed from their origin. Often, they bore symbols advertising the most notable commodity or achievement of the issuing city or authority. Sometimes, as in the case of posthumous Alexander types and the ubiquitous owls of Athens, they simply beat on a familiar and comfortable drum.

Several of these trading centers became major metropolitan areas, eventually leading to colonization and to the development of resources far beyond their original borders. Much of the history of the Greeks is a

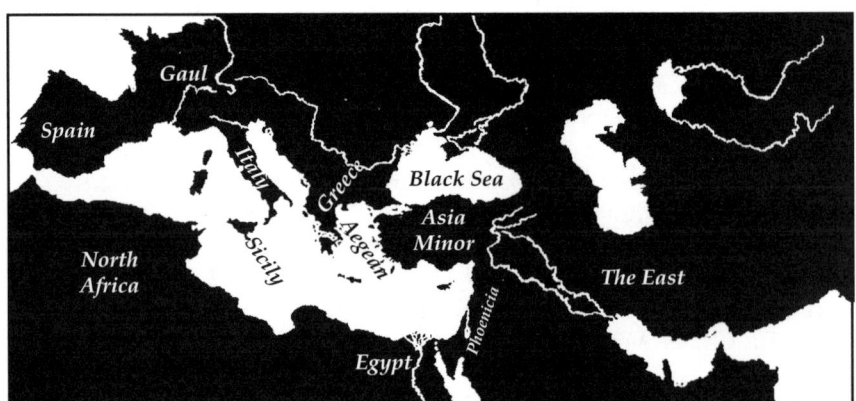

reflection of conflicts between these city-states and their neighbors. Sometimes they joined in a league or federation to assist in mutual defense. These leagues issued federal currency for use among themselves, and the resulting series are very collectable from an historic point of view. Often, the prosperity of a region can be tied to the successful conclusion of prolonged conflict.

Distribution patterns of coinage were also affected by conflicts. One of the important reasons for striking coins in large numbers was to pay mercenaries who supported the cause of a particular city or king. The payment of tribute also demanded huge quantities of precious metal coinage. Mercenaries not only spent their earnings while on campaign, but like any modern soldier they tended to save for a better life after the conflict. Since mercenaries were often drawn from far corners of the ancient world, coinage of the employer made its way to places where trade was not necessarily important. One of the great advantages of the standardized imagery on Alexander tetradrachms was that a mercenary could spend it in a multitude of places without difficulty—surely no one would deny it!

The cultural brilliance that we generally associate with ancient Greece tended to shine more brightly at some times than at others. Being that coins reflect artistically the psyche of a culture, we can see that ebb and flow in the coins that were issued. The methods of ancient coin production are discussed more fully in Volume I of this series, but we should reiterate that ancient coins were struck by hand, one at a time, and their beauty is often a function of the care taken in production as well as the artistic achievement of the celator. The purpose of issue would naturally have had a noticeable effect on the quality of a mint's product.

On the following pages are brief historical synopses of a few of the major Greek city-states or regions. These vignettes are not intended as a study of Greek history, but simply as a backdrop to understanding the setting in which Greek coinage evolved. Neither is the section complete by any means. This is an overview, and is provided only to illustrate the kinds of coins that were struck by the Greeks. The names of these places will often be seen on the coins themselves in the form of inscriptions. The traditional form for these inscriptions was to record the name of the people in the genitive plural. For example, coins of Syracuse bear the inscription ΣΥΡΑΚΟΣΙΩΝ, and of Thasos as ΘΑΣΙΩΝ. There are, however, exceptions to the rule. Another convention was to record only the first few letters of the place name, like ΑΘΕ for Athens. This is especially true on the earliest coins of each city. There are many other reasons for inscriptions appearing on a coin, and most have a readily apparent meaning. The names of gods or heroes, and personal epithets, are among the most often seen, but mint control symbols and magisterial monograms are also common.

The arrangement of cities or regions in this section roughly follows the long established method developed by Eckhel in the 18th century. This is also the arrangement used by most auction cataloguers. It is based on a geographical ordering which starts at the northwest corner of the Mediterranean and proceeds eastward across Italy and Greece into Asia Minor. It then follows the coastline through ancient Judaea to Egypt and westward through North Africa back to the Pillars of Herakles (Straits of Gibraltar). Coins of the Baktrian Greeks and other Eastern dominions follow after those of the Mediterranean rim countries. Our categories labeled "League Coinage" and "Island Greeks" do not fit into any established scheme, but are grouped in that manner only for convenience. Consequently, bibliographic references in these sections may serve more than one geographic region.

It is not possible to describe or illustrate here coins from all of the Greek cities, nor even those of the first rank. Again, what we have included is intended only as an introduction, and is merely representative of what one will find in the coinage of various regions. When appropriate, we have also included at the end of each section a fairly comprehensive list of the cities which struck coinage in Greek times.

BIBLIOGRAPHY
The World of the Greeks

Anthony, John. *Collecting Greek Coins*, New York, 1983.
Boardman, John. *The Greeks Overseas*, Penguin, 1973.
Boardman, John; Jasper Griffin and Oswyn Murray. *Greece and the Hellenistic World*, Oxford, 1988.
Carradice, I.A. and M. J. Price. *Coinage in the Greek World*, London, 1988.
Casson, Lionel. *Travel in the Ancient World*, Toronto, 1974.
Graham, A.J. *Colony and Mother City in Ancient Greece*, Manchester University Press, 1964.
Grant, Michael. *The Rise of the Greeks*, New York, 1988.
Jenkins, G.K. *Ancient Greek Coins*, London, 1990.
Klawans, Zander H. *Handbook of Ancient Greek and Roman Coins*, Whitman, Racine WI, 1995.
Sear, David. *Greek Coins and Their Values*, 2 vols., London, 1978.
Seltman, Charles. *Greek Coins*, London, 1977.
Tameanko, Marvin. "Coins reveal the extensive explorations of the ancient Phoenicians", *The Celator*, Vol. 6, No. 8, August 1992.
Vagi, David L. "Early Greek coinage spread from Ionia to Italy", *The Celator*, Vol. 8, No. 4, April 1994.

Western Mediterranean

BARKIDS: Hamilkar Barka established the Carthaginian presence in Spain during a nine year campaign. Following his death, his son Hasdrubal assumed command of the forces there. The latter died during a campaign into Italy to assist his brother Hannibal. An interesting series of coins struck by the Barkids in Spain includes one bearing a portrait thought to be that of Hasdrubal.

Barkids, Hasdrubal? AR shekel, ca. 228 BC

EBUSUS: To the east of Spain lies the island group known as the Balearics. Among them is Ebusus. During the 3rd to 2nd centuries BC this island issued a bronze coin bearing the peculiar representation of the Kabeiros. This mystic divinity (actually a group of four divinities) was associated in early mythology with the creation and ordering of the universe, and was worshipped in connection with the harvest.

Ebusus, Balearic islands AE 17, ca. 3rd-2nd C. BC

MASSALIA: Phokians founded this city on the southern coast of Gaul about 600 BC. It remained independent throughout the Greek period, even resisting the Carthaginians. An excellent harbor supported a defensive fleet and prosperous trade. The Romans allowed Massalians to retain its independence until the Civil Wars.

Massalia, Gaul, AR obol after ca. 400 BC

Mint Cities of Spain

Abdera	Ebura Cerealis	Obulco
Bilbilis	Ebusus, Balearics	Osca
Calagurris	Emporiai	Rhoda
Carteia	Ercavica	Saetabis
Carthago Nova	Gades	Saguntum
Cascantum	Ilerda	Segobriga
Castulo	Iliberis	Sexsi
Celsa	Malaca	Tarraco
Corduba	Numantia	Turiaso
		Valentia

Magna Graecia / Italy

The term Magna Graecia (Greater Greece) was a name given in ancient times to the districts in southern Italy inhabited by the Greeks. Some of the cities normally included in this region are: Taras, Sybaris, Kroton, Kaulonia, Herakleia, Metapontum, Lokroi, Rhegion, Cumae and Neapolis. There were, of course, many other cities in Italy which were inhabited by Greeks—see the chart which follows. The history of the region is dominated by the frequent incursion of Carthaginians and Romans.

CUMAE was the oldest of the Greek colonies in Magna Graecia, and from it many of the other important cities of Italy and Sicily were founded. It was supposedly the residence of the earliest Sibyl, a name given to a group of prophetic women.

At HERAKLEIA, Pyrrhos won a victory against the Romans in 280. The coins of this city often depict the hero for which it is named. On the nomos shown here, the weight of Herakles is supported on one leg in the manner of Polykleitos' Doryphoros.

KAULONIA: The coins of this city often place Apollo in the presence of a stag. The stag was an attribute of his sister Artemis, and the two were often worshipped together.

KROTON was a center of worship to Apollo, and the Delphic tripod was a frequent motif on the city's coins. On the silver nomos shown here, Nike places a wreath on the tripod—perhaps an allusion to Kroton's Olympic victories.

Cumae, Campania
AR nomos, ca. 430-420 BC

Herakleia, Lucania
AR nomos, ca. 300-280

Kaulonia, Bruttium
AR nomos, ca. 440-390 BC

Kroton, Bruttium
AR nomos, ca 420-340 BC

LOKROI EPIZEPHYRIOI: This Italian city was settled by Lokrians from mainland Greece. The fourth century staters of this city are among the most artistic of the coins struck in southern Italy. The eagle and hare motif of Akragas fame is repeated here, opposite a powerful head of Zeus.

Lokroi Epizephyrioi, Bruttium
AR stater, ca. 350-300 BC

At RHEGION, opposite the Sicilian city of Messana, a facing lion head of exquisite workmanship graced fifth century tetradrachm reverses. On the obverse of these coins one finds an interesting variety of Apollo heads, mostly executed with great sensitivity.

Rhegion, Bruttium
AR tetradrachm, ca. 435-425 BC

TARAS: Among new collectors, one of the most popular Greek coins is the "Boy on a Dolphin" type from Taras (Roman Tarentum). The massive issue of coinage from this city boasts more variety of detail than practically any other in the Greek series.

Taras, Calabria
AR nomos, ca. 334-330 BC

BIBLIOGRAPHY
Magna Graecia / Italy

Brauer, George. T*aras, Its History and Coinage*, New Rochelle, 1986.
Holloway, Ross R. *Art and Coinage in Magna Graecia*, 1978.
Holloway, R and G.K. Jenkins. *Terina*, Bellinzona, 1983.
Ravel, O. *Descriptive Catalogue of the Collection of Tarentine Coins formed by M.P. Vlasto*, London, 1947 (1977 Obol reprint).
Rutter, N.K. *Campanian Coinages, 475-380 BC*, Edinburgh, 1979.
Sambon, Arthur. *Les monnaies antiques de l'Italie*, Paris, 1903.
Scheu, Frederick. "The Coinage of the Lucanians", *Numismatic Chronicle*, 1964.
Williams, R. *The Silver Coinage of Velia*, London, 1992

Mint Cities of Italy

Apulia, Arpi
Apulia, Ausculum
Apulia, Azetium
Apulia, Barium
Apulia, Butuntum
Apulia, Caelia
Apulia, Canusium
Apulia, Hyrium / Uria
Apulia, Luceria
Apulia, Neapolis
Apulia, Rubi
Apulia, Salapia
Apulia, Teate
Apulia, Venusia
Bruttium, Heiponion
Bruttium, Kaulonia
Bruttium, Konsentia
Bruttium, Kroton
Bruttium, Lokroi Epizephyrioi
Bruttium, Mesma
Bruttium, Mystia and Hyporon
Bruttium, Nuceria
Bruttium, Pandosia
Bruttium, Petelia
Bruttium, Rhegion
Bruttium, Terina
Bruttium, Vibo Valentia
Calabria, Brundisium
Calabria, Graxa
Calabria, Hyria / Orra
Calabria, Sturnium
Calabria, Taras
Calabria, Uxentum
Campania, Allifae
Campania, Atella
Campania, Calatia
Campania, Cales
Campania, Capua
Campania, Compulteria
Campania, Dymai
Campania, Fenseris
Campania, Hyria
Campania, Kymai
Campania, Neapolis
Campania, Nola
Campania, Nuceria Alfaterna
Campania, Phistelia
Campania, Suessa Aurunca
Campania, Teanum Sidicinum
Etruria, Peithesa
Etruria, Populonia
Etruria, Thezi / Thezle
Etruria, Velathri (Olaterrae)
Etruria, Volsinii
Frentani, Frentrum
Frentani, Larinum
Latium, Alba Fucens
Latium, Aquinum
Latium, Signia
Lucania, Copia
Lucania, Herakleia
Lucania, Laos
Lucania, Metapontum
Lucania, Paestum
Lucania, Poseidonia
Lucania, Siris and Pyxos
Lucania, Sybaris
Lucania, Thourioi
Lucania, Velia
Picenum, Ancona
Picenum, Hatria
Samnium, Aesernia
Samnium, Aquilonia
Samnium, Beneventum
Umbria, Ariminum
Umbria, Iguvium
Umbria, Tuder

Sicily

Sicily derived its name from a tribe of early inhabitants, the Siceli. The soil of the region is very fertile, and it was a great producer of wheat and other agricultural products. The coinage of Sicily is perhaps the most artistic of all Greek coinage. From the sixth century until the Roman occupation, Sicily consistently produced coinage of unsurpassed beauty and celatorial excellence. This in spite of 150 years of conflict with and occupation by the military forces of Carthage. The coins of Sicily will be seen throughout this volume, especially in the sections dealing with signed dies and Masterpieces of Greek Art.

NAXOS: This city, the oldest Greek settlement in Sicily, was founded in 735 BC by the Chalcideans. It was also the issuer of Sicily's first coinage. The city prospered from the production of wine and it is not surprising that they should have honored Dionysos on their first issue. Naxos was destroyed in 403 BC by Dionysios, the tyrant of Syracuse. In 358, its surviving inhabitants founded the city of Tauromenion.

Naxos, AR drachm, ca. 550-530 BC

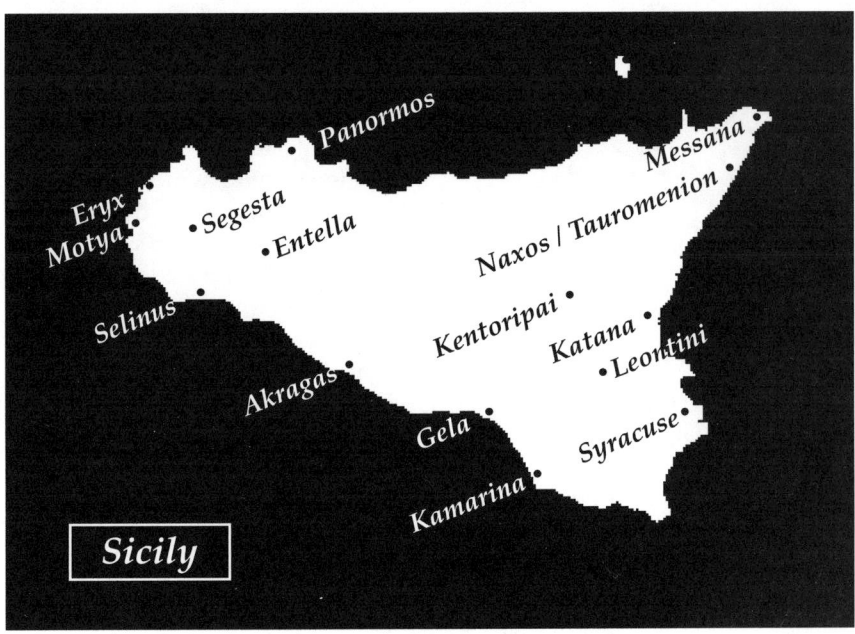

Sicily

*Gela, AR didrachm (x2)
ca. 490-475 BC*

GELA: Founded by Rhodians from Lindos, this city was originally named Lindii. It was located on the banks of the Gelas river and the local river god is depicted on the city's coins from a very early period. Gela was the last home of Aeschylus, and an important center until the tyrant Gelon relocated half of the city's inhabitants to Syracuse. It fell into decay—and was totally uninhabited by the time of Augustus.

*Katana, AR tetradrachm
ca. 420 BC*

KATANA was an important city at the foot of Mt. Aitna, founded in 730 BC by residents of Naxos. It was taken and repopulated as Aitna in 476 by Hieron I, but was regained by the original inhabitants about ten years later. Several master engravers worked at Katana toward the end of the fifth century. The city fell under Roman control during the first Punic War.

*Messana, AR tetradrachm
ca. 430-420 BC*

MESSANA: This city holds a strategic position on the strait separating Sicily from Italy (only four miles wide at this point). It has a sickle shaped harbor and was originally called Zankle, which is a pun on its shape. Anaxilaos drove out the Samians and resettled the city with Messenians, naming it Messana. The city was taken and destroyed by the Carthaginians in 396. It was rebuilt by Dionysios and in 312 fell into the hands of Agathokles who quartered Mamertini in the city. On the death of Agathokles, these Campanian mercenaries took over the city, killed all of the male inhabitants, and took their wives and property. A war broke out between them and Hieron of Syracuse, during which Carthage and Rome clashed while both were giving aid to Messana. This led to the first Punic War.

PANORMOS: The excellent harbor at Panormos served as headquarters for the Carthaginian fleet in Sicily. The city was founded originally by Phoenicians, and local inhabitants were probably not opposed to the Carthaginian presence. The city fell to the Romans in 254 BC during the first Punic War. The coin illustrated here was struck under Roman control of the city, and depicts the typically Roman deity Janus.

Panormos, AE 23mm after 241 BC

PYRRHOS: The King of Epeiros claimed to be a descendent of Achilles and, for a time, seemed to be invulnerable in battle himself. He is one of the most famous soldiers of fortune ever to live. Pyrrhos fought with valor alongside Demetrios Poliorketes at Ipsos, and

Pyrrhos, AE 22mm, 278-276 BC

later went as a hostage for Demetrios to Egypt. There, he married the daughter of Berenike. Supplied with a fleet and ground forces by Ptolemy, he returned to Epeiros. Shortly thereafter, he drove Demetrios out of Macedon, and ruled jointly for a short time with Lysimachos before being deposed. In 280, he answered a request for aid from the Tarentines, and crossed into Italy to oppose the Romans. He conducted two campaigns against Rome, one taking him to within 24 miles of the city, but was unable to force a peace. At this time he received a request from the Greeks in Sicily to help them repel the Carthaginians. It was during his two year campaign in Sicily that the bronze coin illustrated here was struck. This enterprise also fell short of its aims and Pyrrhos was forced to retire back to Taras, and finally to Epeiros, with only 40% of his foot soldiers and 15% of his cavalry remaining. He was compelled by the need for funds to invade Macedon, and was successful in defeating Antigonos Gonatas. As King of Macedon for the second time, he found himself in need of further military rewards. He turned against Sparta, and was unsuccessful. Then he moved against Argos and while fighting in the streets he was killed by a tile which a woman threw from the rooftop of a house. In addition to a legend of military adventure and misadventure, Pyrrhos left behind a trail of coins reminding us of his presence.

Mint Cities of Sicily

Abakainon	Hipana	Mytistratos
Adranon	Hybla	Nakona
Agyrion	Iaitia	Naxos
Aitna	Kalakte	Panormos
Akragas	Kamarina	Paropos
Akrai	Katane	Petra
Alaisa	Kentoripai	Phintias
Alontion	Kephaloidion	Piakos
Amestratos	Leontinoi	Sardinia
Assoros	Lilybaion	Segesta
Enna	Longane	Selinus
Entella	Megara Hyblaia	Solus
Eryx	Menainon	Syracuse
Galaria	Messana	Tauromenion
Gela	Morgantina	Thermai
Himera	Motya	Tyndaris
		Zankle / Messana

BIBLIOGRAPHY
Sicily

Arnold-Biucchi, Carmen. *The Randazzo Hoard 1980 and Sicilian Chronology in the Early Fifth Century B.C.*, New York, 1990.
Boehringer, E. *Die Münzen von Syrakus*, Berlin, 1929.
Cahn, Herbert A. *Die Münzen der Sizilischen Stadt Naxos*, Basel, 1944.
Calciati, Romolo. *Corpus Nummorum Siculorum, The Bronze Coinage*, Bologna, 1983.
Hill, G.F. *The Coins of Ancient Sicily*, Westminster, 1903, (Forni reprint).
Jenkins, Kenneth. *Coins of Greek Sicily*, London, 1976.
Jenkins, G.K. *The coinage of Gela*, Berlin, 1970.
Jenkins, G.K. "Coins of Punic Sicily", *Swiss Numismatic Review*, four parts, 1971, 1974, 1977 and 1978.
Kraay, Colin. *The Archaic Coinage of Himera*, London, 1984.
Rizzo, G.E. *Monete greche della Sicilia*, Rome, 1946, (Forni reprint).
Westermark, U. and G.K. Jenkins. *The Coinage of Kamarina*, London, 1980.

Northern Greece / Thrace

Northern Greece was populated mainly by indigenous tribes of mixed descent. The coastal cities were colonized by settlers from established Greek city-states, but the inland areas were slow to adopt Hellenic culture and practices. Their contact with the Greeks was mainly in the form of trade, and the richness of mines in the region made the striking of coins a natural activity. Many of the coins from this region bear images close to nature. Wild animals and Dionysiac references are the most prevalent.

ABDERA was a Thracian town near the mouth of the Nestus river. It was a prosperous city, and the birthplace of many famous philosophers—including Protogoras, the Sophist, who died at Abdera about the year this coin was issued (411). In spite of its famous sons, "Abderan" became, like "Cretan", a proverb for stupidity.

Abdera, AR tetradrachm ca. 411-386 BC

AKANTHOS, located on the Chalkidike Peninsula, was colonized by Greeks from the island of Andros—probably because of its local mines. Coins were issued from as early as the sixth century BC. The lion and bull, sometimes solo and sometimes in combat, figure prominently in coin motifs of this city from the Archaic through the Classical Period.

Akanthos, AR tetradrachm ca. 440 BC

MENDE was a Macedonian city on the west coast of the Pallene peninsula at the widest point of the gulf that terminates at Thessalonika. It was founded by settlers from the city of Eretria, and was famous for its wine. Like many other wine producing regions, Mende honored the god Dionysos on its coins. He is shown here riding on the back of a donkey and holding a kantharos of wine.

Mende, AR tetradrachm ca. 460-423 BC

MARONEIA was also famous for its wine. Like Mende, this Thracian city also honored Dionysos on its coinage. The city was colonized by Greeks from the island of Chios, itself a noted wine producing region. During the mid-second century, when large flan tetradrachms were being produced throughout the Hellenic world, Maroneia issued an attractive design with the head of Dionysos crowned by a wreath of ivy. Original dies of this type were carved by master celators, but the series degenerated as local craftsmen inexpertly copied the theme.

Maroneia, Thrace
AR tetradrachm, after 148 BC

THE BISALTI were a Thracian people, who lived on the west bank of the Strymon river. Although settled in a district of Macedonia, they were independent and subject to their own prince until the Persian invasion of 480. The coinage of this tribe and of their neighbors—the Derrones, Ichnai, Edones, Orreskioi, Zaielioi, Pernaioi, Dionysioi and Laiai—is referred to as "Thraco-Macedonian." The fractional coinage of this region is particularly interesting, with many uncertain types and a wide range of subjects. For the collector who enjoys research and the challenge of a good mystery, there are coins in this series which will certainly qualify.

The Bisalti,
AR octadrachm
ca. 480 BC

DAMASTION was the political center of one of the richest silver producing districts of northern Greece. It was located in the Illyro-Paeonian region, but the actual site of the city has never been found. Little is known about the entire area. It was the home of independent kings, and was apparently wealthy, but the historical record leaves us only with scant information—mostly about the interests of Philip II in local silver mines. Damastion produced a series of severe but attractive coins during the fourth century.

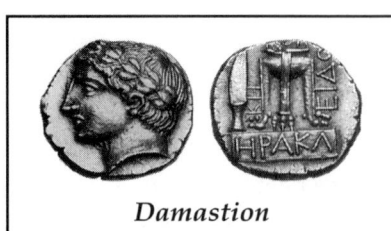

Damastion
AR tetradrachm, ca. 360-345 BC

The Macedonian Kingdom

Macedon was located in north central Greece, bounded on the south by Mt. Olympos, and on the east by the river Strymon—which flows north to south between this region and Thrace. The Macedonian monarchy was said to be founded by the descendants of Temenus, one of the Heraclidae who invaded the Peloponnesos and was later driven out of Argos. They are therefore referred to as the Temenids.

The first Macedonian king to issue coinage was Alexander I, who ruled from 495 to 454 BC. In the year 480, Alexander was obliged to join Xerxes as the Persians invaded Greece. He was sympathetic to the Greeks, however, and warned them the night before the battle of Plataea.

Alexander I
AR tetradrachm, 498-454 BC

The kingdom was expanded greatly by Philip II, who acceded in 359. He had ambitions of conquering Asia, but was cut short by an assassin. His son, Alexander III, carried out that dream. For more on Alexander, and the Macedonian successors, see the portrait section later

Philip II,
AR tetradrachm, 359-336 BC

in this volume. Philip did, however, conquer most of Greece, and obtained recognition of the Macedonians as "true Greeks".

Following the death of Alexander, there was a period of turmoil in which several of his successors tried to claim the Macedonian throne. Virtually all of these rulers struck coinage, which reflects the history of the period down to the Roman conquest in 168 BC. In spite of the growing popularity of regal portraits, not all of these rulers struck portrait coins.

Emerging from this conflict as the undisputed King of Macedon, and securing the claim of the Antigonid Dynasty, was Demetrios Poliorketes. Among the enemies that he overcame was Ptolemy of Egypt, whose fleet he defeated at Salamis. The event was commemorated on a tetradrachm depicting Nike, standing on the prow of a ship and blowing the horn of victory. On the reverse, Poseidon stands in a majestic pose with trident raised. The allusion to Demetrios' naval accomplishment is unmistakable.

Antigonos II Gonatas, "knock-kneed", (277-239 BC) was the son of Demetrios Poliorketes. He regained the throne following an interregnum of 11 years, and restored Antigonid rule to Macedon. There are not any portrait coins known of this king, but it was suggested by Imhoof-Blumer *(Monnaies Grecques)* that the head of Pan, on certain dies, is portrayed bearing the features of Antigonos. Jenkins *(Ancient Greek Coins)* regards this speculation as "idle". Pan was incorporated as a motif in honor of his supposed assistance in the campaign of Antigonos against the Gauls.

Antigonos Doson, a relative of Gonatas who ruled on behalf of the young Philip V, also commemorated a naval victory on his coins. The combination of Poseidon (obverse) and Apollo on an impressive tetradrachm alludes to the victory of the Antigonids and Seleukids over the Ptolemaic fleet at Andros.

After the disaster at Kynoskephalai, where Roman forces annihilated the Macedonians, the dynasty was mortally weakened. Autonomous coins were issued at many cities from this period on.

Demetrios Poliorketes,
AR tetradrachm, ca. 294-293 BC

Antigonos Gonatas,
AR tetradrachm, 277-239 BC

Antigonos Doson,
AR tetradrachm. 229-221 BC

Autonomous, AE 24mm,
ca. 185-165 BC

The World of Alexander

The entire world, in every age, has held a fascination for Alexander III (the Great) from Macedon. This conqueror of legendary achievement is known to every school child, even in our age of apathy toward ancient history. His exploits are so well documented that it is unnecessary to relate them here. Anyone wishing to read about Alexander can obtain a wealth of material from any library or from any encyclopedia.

The coinage of Alexander is quite interesting. The standard gold staters with the helmeted head of Athena and a standing Nike circulated in huge numbers throughout the entire ancient world. Likewise, the silver tetradrachm with Herakles wearing a lion's skin and Zeus seated on a throne could be found everywhere. Although not very exciting artistically, this standardization was a practical accommodation to the needs of standing armies and the huge bureaucracy needed to run an empire of that magnitude. For this purpose, he could have selected no better images. These types were so well accepted that they were

Alexander III
AV stater, 336-323 BC

Alexander III
AR tetradrachm, 336-323 BC

imitated even by those who did not fall under the Macedonian's direct control. Fractional silver and bronze received less attention, with local coinage often continuing to serve the needs of internal commerce.

As important as these standard issues were, they were not the only coins struck under Alexander's authority. Multiples in gold and silver (including a dekadrachm) were issued primarily for special occasions. At Babylon, the traditional type of Baal seated on a throne, with a lion reverse, was retained. Alexander must have seen the value of allowing local customs to survive. The conquered citizens of Babylon could easily tolerate a new king, they had seen many

Babylon, AR tetradrachm
under Alexander, 328-323 BC

33

before, but it would not be easy to supplant their cultural and religious traditions. Of course, for Greeks who might question such an accommodation, it was easy enough to see in the figure of Baal a seated Zeus—not unlike that on Alexander's tetradrachms. The Persian lion was easily enough perceived as a symbol of conquest. In fact, some liberties were taken in the portrayal of Zeus even on the tetradrachms. At least one Asian mint issued a tetradrachm with Zeus wearing a Persian headdress! As the empire grew larger and larger, Alexander allowed for greater and greater freedoms of this sort. He actually styled himself after "The Great King" of the East, and married Roxana, the daughter of the King of Sogdiana. He also encouraged his officers to marry aristocratic ladies of the Eastern courts. Meanwhile, he left behind a bureaucratic system that was well suited to the demands of occupation, and which produced a massive coinage to sustain that system.

One of the most famous of the "nonstandard" issues is a mysterious silver dekadrachm known from less than ten specimens. In 327-325 BC Alexander conducted a campaign into India, extending his rule to the lower Indus. During this campaign, Alexander was challenged by Poros, the king of Paurava. He routed the elephants of Poros at the battle of Hydaspes and overran the Punjab. Although virtually unopposed, his army balked at further penetration into India, ending their seemingly invincible advance. Apparently in commemoration of this victory, Alexander issued a large silver coin which depicts him mounted on Bucephalus, his faithful steed, charging against a retreating war elephant—ostensibly carrying Poros and his mahout. On the reverse of this coin we find Alexander standing frontally in a Greek cavalry uniform. He wears a crested Phrygian helmet with a tall feather (described by Plutarch as having been worn by Alexander at the battle of the Granicus). He holds a spear in his left hand and a thunderbolt in his right. The thunderbolt represents Alexander's claimed descent from Zeus. According to Pliny, a contemporary painting by Apelles also portrayed Alexander holding a thunderbolt. A sword hangs at his side, and above Alexander is crowned by a flying Nike.

Alexander III, AR (Poros) dekadrachm, ca. 327/6 BC

Mint Cities of Northern Greece

Illyro-Paeonian Region, Damastion
Illyro-Paeonian Region, Daparria
Illyro-Paeonian Region, Darado
Illyro-Paeonian Region, Nikarchos
Illyro-Paeonian Region, Pelagia
Illyro-Paeonian Region, Simon
Macedon, Aigai
Macedon, Aineia
Macedon, Akanthos
Macedon, Amphaxitis
Macedon, Amphipolis
Macedon, Aphytis
Macedon, Eion
Macedon, Herakleia Sintika
Macedon, Lete
Macedon, Mende
Macedon, Methone
Macedon, Neapolis
Macedon, Olophyxos
Macedon, Olynthos
Macedon, Orthagoreia
Macedon, Pelagonia
Macedon, Pella
Macedon, Philippi
Macedon, Potidaia
Macedon, Pydna
Macedon, Sermylia
Macedon, Skione
Macedon, Spartolos
Macedon, Terone
Macedon, Therma
Macedon, Tragilos
Macedon, Uranopolis
Thrace, Abdera
Thrace, Agathopolis
Thrace, Aigospotamoi
Thrace, Ainos
Thrace, Alopekonnesos
Thrace, Bisanthe
Thrace, Byzantion
Thrace, Dikaia
Thrace, Elaious
Thrace, Kardia
Thrace, Krithote
Thrace, Kypsela
Thrace, Lysimacheia
Thrace, Madytos
Thrace, Maroneia
Thrace, Perinthos
Thrace, Selymbria
Thrace, Sestos

BIBLIOGRAPHY
Northern Greece / Thrace

Bellinger, A. *Essays on the Coinage of Alexander The Great*, New York, 1963.
Price, Martin J. *Coins of the Macedonians*, London, 1974.
May, J.M.F. *The Coinage of Damastion*, 1939; *Ainos, its History and Coinage*, 1950; *The Coinage of Abdera, 540-345 B.C.*, 1966 (all at London).
LeRider, G. *Le Monnayage d'Argent et d'Or de Philippe II*, Paris, 1977.
Lorber, C. *Amphipolis-The Civic Coinage in Silver and Gold*, Los Angeles, 1990.
Price, Martin J. *The Coinage in the Name of Alexander the Great and Philip Arrhidaeus, A British Museum Catalog*, Zürich/London, 1991.
Raymond, Doris. *Macedonian Regal Coinage to 413 B.C.*, New York, 1953.
Thompson, Margaret. *Alexander's Drachm Mints, Vol. I: Sardes and Miletus*, ANS Numismatic Studies 16, New York, 1983.

Western/Central Greece

AMBRACIA ("A" in the field) was a colony of Corinth founded in Epeiros, about 660 BC. It became the capital of King Pyrrhos, and later a member of the Aitolian League. It was taken by the Romans in 189 BC.

Ambracia, AR stater ca. 404-360 BC

LEUKAS ("Λ" in the field) was another of the many Corinthian colonies in western Greece. Originally a peninsula, it became an island by virtue of a man-made canal. A famous temple of Apollo marked the spot where the Lyric poet Sappho supposedly leaped to her death from a cliff high above the sea.

Leukas, AR stater ca. 405-345 BC

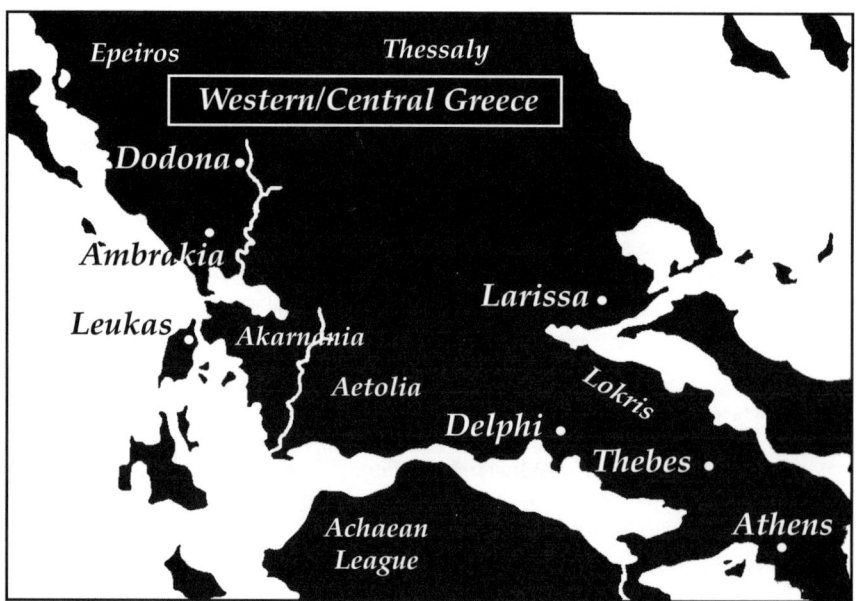

DELPHI: The oracle of Apollo Delphinios (hence the dolphins on this coin) was the most celebrated in the ancient world. The temple treasury, and individual city treasuries at Delphi, were swelled with offerings and deposits from all parts of the Greek world. It was originally called Pytho and was the site of the Pythian games which were conducted by the Amphiktyonic council.

Delphi, Phokis
AR trihemiobol (x2), ca. 360 BC

LARISSA: The facing heads of Larissa have been regarded by many as being derived from the Syracusan tetradrachm by Kimon. This is probably true in the sense that all art is influenced by what has come before—but it is not likely that there is any direct

Larissa, Thessaly
AR didrachm, ca. 344-321 BC

correlation, similarities notwithstanding. Within the Larissan series there are many differing treatments of the facing head. All of them are similar in some way to something that has preceded them.

THEBES: This chief city of Boeotia was settled very early by the Phoenicians, and it was here that the Phoenician alphabet was first introduced to the Greeks. The city played an important role in mythology, as the birthplace of both Dionysos and Herakles. In Greek literature it

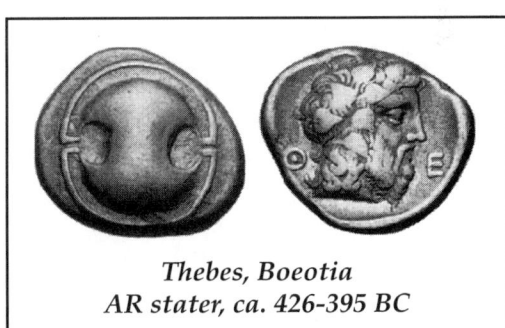

Thebes, Boeotia
AR stater, ca. 426-395 BC

was the scene of the tragedy of "Oedipus" and also of the "Seven against Thebes" and its sequel—the revenge of the Epigoni. The city was ruled by an oligarchy until near the end of the Peloponnesian War when it became a democracy and remained so until Roman times. Theban defeat of the Spartans in 371 made it the most powerful of all Greek states until the rise of Philip II and his son Alexander.

League Coinage

There were many leagues or confederations among ancient Greek cities due to the fact that alone they were relatively weak. The purposes of these organizations varied, but many of them cooperated economically as well as militarily. Coinage issued by the league was accepted among all members, and sometimes cities used only the league coinage, foregoing their own types. Included here are some very brief descriptions of leagues which struck coinage from time to time. It is not a comprehensive list, but includes those whose coins are seen frequently in today's collector market.

The Amphiktyones were a very ancient league of twelve cities in central Greece, organized to protect the sanctuaries of Apollo at Delphi and Demeter at Anthela. They controlled the Pythian games, held every four years, and maintained a sort of nonaggression pact among themselves.

Amphiktyonic League AR stater, ca. 336-334 BC

The Achaean League was made up originally of towns on the northwest coast of the Peloponnesos, but grew in the third century to encompass nearly all of southern Greece. It was most active in opposing Macedonian expansionism. League coinage was struck at virtually all of the member cities.

Achaean League, AR triobol ca. 222 BC

The Aitolian League was formed in 338 BC also to counter the growing influence of Philip II after the battle of Chaeronea. The participating towns were in western Greece from Akarnania to Epeiros. In 189 BC, the league signed a treaty with Rome which ended its existence.

Aitolian League, AR didrachm 260-220 BC

While the leagues already mentioned were primarily organized to counter a Macedonian threat, the Arkadian cities had earlier faced the specter of aggression from Sparta. They finally enjoyed some security after the battle of Leuctra in 371 where Epaminondas and his Theban forces crushed the Spartans.

Arkadian League, AR obol, ca. 4th century BC

Boeotia was divided into 14 separate states which formed a league with Thebes as its capital. The magistrates of the confederacy were called Boeotarchs, and were elected annually.

Boeotian League AR hemidrachm, ca 338-315 BC

The Bretti, sometimes called Brutti, were an inland group of rebel Lucanians who allied themselves and supported Hannibal in the Second Punic War. After the defeat of the Carthaginians, they lost their independence and were treated savagely by the Romans. At the time of Hannibalic occupation, they produced some lovely coins

Brettian League, AE sextens 215-205 BC

with interesting motifs. The type illustrated here features Ares wearing an ornamented helmet and the unusual deity Hera Hoplosmia, patroness of the Hoplite warrior.

The Euboean city of Chalkis founded so many cities on the peninsulas between the Thermaic gulf and the river Strymon that the whole region was known as Chalkidike. The cities of this region were banded together in a league that prospered until its capital, Olynthos, fell to Philip II of Macedon in 348 BC.

Chalkidian League AR tetradrachm, ca. 350 BC

The Euboian League, an alliance of towns on the largest of the Aegean islands, was formed in 411 BC with Eretria as its capital. The league issued silver coinage to 267 BC.

Following the Macedonian conquest, Lycia fell to the Seleukids and then the Rhodians. They were restored to independence by the Romans, and formed a league of 23 cities which maintained their own governments. A chief magistrate presided over the federal council. It lasted into the reign of Claudius.

The Thessalian League was a loose confederacy of feudal like states run by a few great Thessalian families. In times of need, they elected a chief magistrate called a Tagus. The seat of the Thessalian diet was Larissa.

Euboian League, AR drachm ca. 322/317-307 BC

Lycian League, AR hemidrachm 1st century BC

Thessalian League AR double victoriatus, 99/8 BC

BIBLIOGRAPHY

League Coinage

Clerk, M.G. *Catalogue of the Coins of the Achaean League*, London, 1895.
Kinns, Philip. "The Amphictionic Coinage Reconsidered", *NC*, 1983.
Picard, O. *Chalcis et la Conféderation Eubéen*, Paris, 1979.
Raven, E.J.P. "The Amphictionic Coinage of Delphi, 336-334 B.C.", *Numismatic Chronicle*, 1950.
Roberts, W. Rhys and Barclay V. Head. *The Ancient Boeotians and The Coinage of Boeotia*, consolidated edition, Ares, Chicago, 1974.
Robinson, D.M. and P. Clement. *The Chalkidic Mint*, Baltimore, 1938.
Thompson, M. *The Agrinion Hoard*, ANS NNM 159, New York, 1968.
Troxell, H.A. *The Coinage of the Lycian League*, ANS NNM 162, 1982.
Wallace, W.P. *The Euboian League and its coinage*, ANS NNM 134, 1956.
Warren, J. L. *Greek Federal Coinage*, (reprint) Chicago, 1969.
Williams, R. T. *The Confederate Coinage of the Arcadians in the Fifth Century B.C.*, New York, 1965.

Athens

*AR tetradrachm
ca. 500 BC*

*AR tetradrachm
ca. 460 BC*

*AR tetradrachm
after 393 BC*

*AR tetradrachm
ca. 140 BC*

Athens was inhabited in prehistoric times and was a relatively defensible city due to its prominent hills. It did not become a major center until the time of Peisistratus and his sons (560-514 BC), but soon after blossomed as a metropolis of the first rank.

According to myth, the city was given to Athena as patroness and protectress after a contest with Poseidon left her the victor. It was said the gods decreed that the one who produced the gift most useful to man would possess the city. Poseidon struck the ground and created a well of sea water; Athena made the olive tree spring from the ground, and was awarded the prize.

Athens figures prominently in the history of ancient Greece, and was the center of classical culture as well as a great metropolis and military power. The newfound wealth and awakening of spirit following the Persian War made Athens great, and under the leadership of Perikles splendid monuments were commissioned. Having been burnt by the Persians, Athens needed rebuilding and the necessary public works fueled great prosperity. The greatest of all these projects was the decoration of the Parthenon, which was placed under the supervision of Pheidias—perhaps the greatest sculptor of all time. The Athenian pottery industry was particularly successful, and Athenian painted vases were highly valued throughout the Mediterranean. Science, philosophy and the performing arts also flourished, and many of the great literary works which we consider the "classics" were written during this period.

Within a half century, fortunes had reversed and the financial devastation of the Peloponnesian War nearly ruined the city.

Still, the period between these two wars was a golden age that few cultures have eclipsed. In spite of the city's great losses, it remained important into Roman times.

A half century ago it was believed that the earliest coins of Athens were silver didrachms bearing an amphora on the obverse and an incuse punch on the reverse. These Seltman "Group A" coins were dated to about 610 BC. They have now been reassigned to the island of Andros and dated to ca. 550-520. The earliest coins of Athens now are believed to be a series struck in the mid sixth century, but with a variety of heraldic devices. These coins, referred to as "Wappenmünzen" were formerly disassociated, but have now been linked by the discovery of common reverse dies and reattributed to Athens.

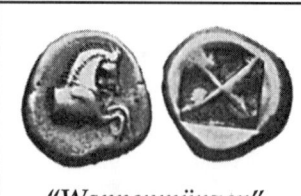

"Wappenmünzen"
AR didrachm, ca. 550 BC

Athenian "owl"
ca. 449 BC

The most famous coins from Athens, and most popular among collectors, were first struck late in the sixth century. They bear the helmeted head of Athena on the obverse and a standing owl on the reverse. This motif became the hallmark of the city and was retained on Athenian coinage for more than 400 years. During this period, artistic style changed dramatically, but the theme persisted. Although the motif is one of the most conservative in the Greek series, it is instructive to compare the images on coins struck over such a long period of time.

Athens, AR didrachm, ca. 465 BC (1.25x)

Athens, AE 14mm, 3rd-1st c. BC

Athens, AE 18mm, 3rd-1st c. BC

About the same time that Syracuse issued the "Demareteion" dekadrachm, Athens had its own impressive ten-drachm coin. It is one of the most desirable, and rarest, coins in the entire Greek series. Babelon hypothesized that this was a "victory" coinage issued after Plataea. Seltman found a reasonable explanation for its issue in the words of Herodotus. In his view, the Athenians benefited greatly from silver extracted from the Laurion mines. At one point they were awarded—instead of being taxed—an annual dole of 10 drachms. Due to the scarcity of one-drachm pieces, it was difficult to make change in the amount of ten. Therefore, two denominations were added, the dekadrachm and the didrachm. The proper change could then be made with two tetradrachms and a didrachm, or a single dekadrachm, or five didrachms. In 483, Themistokles proposed that the dole be given up and the money used to build a fleet to oppose the Persians—hence Seltman's dating to that decade.

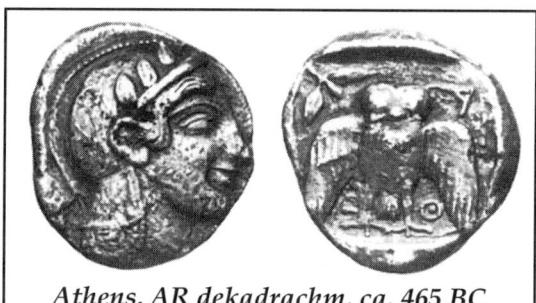

Athens, AR dekadrachm, ca. 465 BC

The pieces have since been reconsidered and a date of 465 has been assigned. It is now believed that these pieces were struck from booty won in the Athenian defeat of the Persian fleet at the Eurymedon River (468 BC), off the coast of Pamphylia in Asia Minor.

BIBLIOGRAPHY

Athens

Haymes, Christopher. "The First Coinage of Athens" *SAN*, Vol. XVIII, No. 2, (May 1991).

Kraay, Colin. "The Archaic Owls of Athens: Classification and Chronology", *Numismatic Chronicle*, 1956.

Kroll, J.H. *The Athenian Agora Volume XXVI: The Greek Coins*, Princeton, 1993.

Seltman, Charles T. *Athens, its History and Coinage Before the Persian Invasion*, Cambridge, 1924.

Starr, Chester G. *Athenian Coinage 480-449 B.C.*, Oxford, 1970.

Svoronos, J.N. *Corpus of the Ancient Coins of Athens*, (a reprint with translations of the 1914 original titled *Trésor des monnaies d'Athènes, Terminé après la mort de l'Auteur*), Ares, 1975.

Thompson, Margaret. *The New Style Silver Coinage of Athens*, New York, 1961.

Aigina

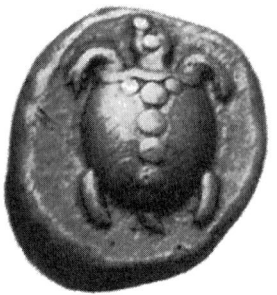

Aigina "Sea Turtle" ca. 480 BC	Aigina "Land Turtle" ca. 350 BC
Aigina, AR stater	

Aigina, an island in the Saronic Gulf only about 15 miles southeast of Athens, obtained its name from the daughter of the river-god Asopos. It was colonized by Dorians from Epidauros and became independent in the sixth century. With independence came commercial prosperity and the island, small as it was, became a powerful city-state in the time prior to the Persian War. They provided 30 ships in the battle against Xerxes at Salamis. Located on the island was one of the earliest mints in Greece proper.

One of the many mysteries of ancient coinage is the design selected for the staters of Aigina. The Aiginetans were sea traders, and the incorporation of a sea turtle as the island's symbol seems to make sense. Why the turtle was changed at some later date to a land species is unknown. It has been conjectured that this reflected the loss of Aigina's maritime trading supremacy following the Peloponnesian War—but this hardly seems likely. Why would a proud people highlight such an unfortunate change of circumstance?

BIBLIOGRAPHY

Aigina

Kollgaard, R. "Coins of Aigina indicate historical and political change", *The Celator*, Vol. 3, No. 5 (May 1989).

Millbank, Samuel R. *The Coinage of Aigina,* ANS Numismatic Notes and Monographs, No. 24.

Wells, H. Bartlett. "Species Indeterminacy in the 'Elder Turtle' Coins of Aigina", *SAN*, Vol. I, No. 4 and Vol. II, No. 1 (April/July 1970).

Mint Cities of Western / Central Greece

Aigina
Akarnania, Alyzia
Akarnania, Anaktorion
Akarnania, Argos Amphilochikon
Akarnania, Astakos
Akarnania, Echinos
Akarnania, Koronta
Akarnania, Medeon
Akarnania, Metropolis
Akarnania, Oiniadai
Akarnania, Stratos
Akarnania, Thyrrheion
Attica, Athens
Attica, Eleusis
Attica, Oropos
Boeotia, Kopai
Boeotia, Koroneia
Boeotia, Lebadeia
Boeotia, Mykalessos
Boeotia, Orchomenos / Erchomenos
Boeotia, Akraiphia
Boeotia, Haliartos
Boeotia, Pharai
Boeotia, Plataia
Boeotia, Tanagra
Boeotia, Thebes
Epeiros, Ambrakia
Epeiros, Dodona
Epeiros, Elea
Epeiros, Kassope
Epeiros, Pandosia
Epeiros, Phoenike
Euboia, Chalkis
Euboia, Eretria
Euboia, Histiaia
Euboia, Karystos
Illyria, Amantia
Illyria, Apollonia
Illyria, Byllis
Illyria, Epidamnos-Dyrrhachium
Lokris Opuntia, Opus
Lokris Opuntia, Skarphea
Lokris Opuntia, Thronion
Lokris Ozolis, Amphissa
Lokris Ozolis, Oiantheia
Megaris, Megara
Phokis, Antikyra
Phokis, Delphi
Phokis, Elateia
Phokis, Ledon
Phokis, Lilaia
Thessaly, Atrax
Thessaly, Demetrias
Thessaly, Ekkarra
Thessaly, Eurea
Thessaly, Eurymenai
Thessaly, Gomphi / Philippopolis
Thessaly, Gonnos
Thessaly, Gyrton
Thessaly, Halos
Thessaly, Herakleia Trachinia
Thessaly, Hypata
Thessaly, Kierion
Thessaly, Krannon
Thessaly, Lamia
Thessaly, Larissa
Thessaly, Larissa Kremaste
Thessaly, Meliboea
Thessaly, Melitaia
Thessaly, Methydrion
Thessaly, Methylion
Thessaly, Metropolis
Thessaly, Mopsion
Thessaly, Orthe
Thessaly, Pelinna
Thessaly, Perrhaebi, The
Thessaly, Phakion
Thessaly, Phalanna
Thessaly, Phaloria
Thessaly, Pharkadon
Thessaly, Pharsalos
Thessaly, Pherai
Thessaly, Proerna
Thessaly, Rhizus
Thessaly, Skotussa
Thessaly, Thebai
Thessaly, Trikka
Illyria, Lissos
Illyria, Orikos
Illyria, Skodra

Peloponnesos

Peloponnesos means "Island of Pelops". That part of Greece south of the Isthmus of Corinth was named for the mythological figure who was a grandson of Zeus, and through his mother Dione a grandson of Atlas as well. He is said to have emigrated from Phrygia with great wealth and settled at Pisa in Elis. There he married Hippodamia, the daughter of King Oenomalis.

Throughout Greek history there was an intense jealousy between cities of the Peloponnesos and those north of the Isthmus. Arising from this envy and mistrust was one of the most famous wars of all time, the Peloponnesian War, which lasted from 431 to 404 BC. Analysis of this war is a classic study in foreign relations, military alliances, defense pacts, and all of the political considerations that modern diplomats and generals face. The masterful history of the war by Thucydides is a standard text book in U.S. Military war colleges to this day. Much of the history of the Peloponnesos is tied into the rivalry between Athens and Sparta which prompted that great war.

CORINTH: Besides controlling the Isthmus between Attica and the Peloponnesos, Corinth derived much of its power and wealth through control of trade in the Western Mediterranean. As a result of colonization and trade agreements, the "Colts of Corinth" became as well known in their own sphere of influence as the Athenian owls were in theirs. Silver staters with the mythological Pegasos flying, and Athena wearing

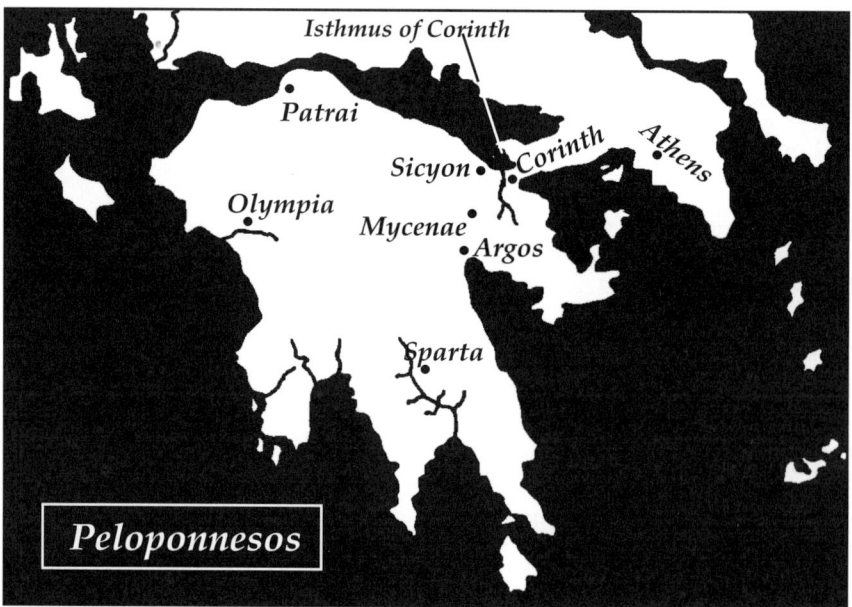

a Corinthian helmet, were issued at Corinth and at a large number of affiliated mints. Those from Corinth herself bear the Greek letter Koppa below Pegasos, while identical types from outlying mints bear a variety of other mint symbols. It was the site of the Isthmian Games, and a major center of commercial pottery production.

Corinth, AR stater, ca. 400-350 BC

ARGOS: The city of Argolis, was one of the most ancient in Greece. According to legend, it was built by the seven Cyclops from Syria. The wolf, a symbol of Apollo Lykios, reflects an active worship of the deity, and there was apparently a temple of Apollo in the Agora. The city was also under the special protection of Hera. She appears also on the coinage of the city in the fifth to fourth centuries. The city of Mycenae, home of King Eurystheus, was also in the Argolid. This was the king that Herakles was bound to serve for twelve years, performing his 12 great labors. It was also the center of Mycenaean civilization, and the home of Agamemnon.

Corinth, AR drachm
ca. 315-310 BC

OLYMPIA: The Peloponnesos provided the setting for the three of the four Pan-Hellenic games. These games rotated annually between four cities. At Delphi, Nemea, Corinth and Olympia, they became the focal point of the Greek world. The most prestigious of these were the Olympic Games. Every four years, Greeks gathered in Elis for this event. Even wars were put on hold for the games to be held. Special coins

Argos, AR hemidrachm
before 146 BC

Olympia, Elis, AR stater, ca. 350 BC

47

were struck at Olympia just for this purpose, and many spectators took them home as souvenirs. The name Elis applied to the whole region, but the city of Elis was founded in 471 BC. Its inhabitants were responsible for maintaining the treasury and conducting the festival at Olympia, where there wasn't any permanent facility or city—only the sanctuary of Zeus. Most of the coins issued at Olympia bear the image of Zeus, or the eagle.

SICYON: Two great artists came from the Peloponnesos: Polykleitos from Argos and Lysippos from Sicyon. This city issued a series of coins depicting the monstrous Chimaera and a dove flying within a wreath—an incongruous pair!

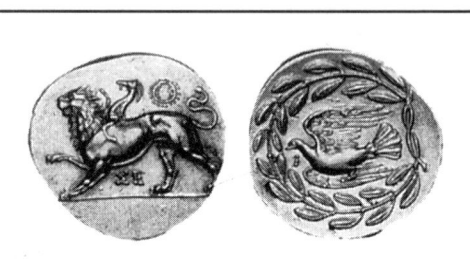

Sicyon, AR stater, ca. 431-400 BC

Mint Cities of the Peloponnesos

Achaia, Aigai	Argolis, Tiryns, Halice	Arkadia, Psophis
Achaia, Aigeira	Argolis, Troizen	Arkadia, Stymphalos
Achaia, Aigion	Arkadia, Alea	Arkadia, Tegea
Achaia, Dyme	Arkadia, Heraia	Arkadia, Thelpusa
Achaia, Patrai	Arkadia, Kaphyai	Corinthia, Corinth
Achaia, Pellene	Arkadia, Kleitor	Elis, Olympia
Argolis, Argos	Arkadia, Mantineia	Elis, Pisa
Argolis, Arsinoe	Arkadia, Megalopolis	Lakonia, Sparta
Argolis, Epidauros	Arkadia, Orchomenos	Messenia, Korone
Argolis, Hermione	Arkadia, Pallantion	Messenia, Messene
Argolis, Kleonai	Arkadia, Parrhasia	Messenia, Thuria
Argolis, Methana	Arkadia, Pheneos	Phliasia, Phlius
		Sikyonia, Sikyon

BIBLIOGRAPHY

Peloponnesos

Calciati, Romolo. *Pegasi*, 2 vols., Mortara, Italy, 1990.
Ravel, Oscar. *Les 'Poulains' de Corinthe, monographie des statéres Corinthiens,* 2 parts, Basel, 1936, 1948.
Seltman, Charles T. *The Temple Coins of Olympia,* New York, 1975.
Warren, Jennifer. "The Autonomous Coinage of Sicyon", *Numismatic Chronicle,* 3 parts, 1983, 1984, 1985.
* for additional references, see the "League Coinage" bibliography.

Island Greeks

CHIOS: This Aegean island, settled by the Ionians, was famous for its wine, figs, marble and pottery. The badge of the city of Chios was the Sphinx, which appears frequently on its coinage and as a stamp on the handle of amphoras bearing wine from Chios. The Sphinx played an important role in the mythical tale of Oedipus (see also Mythology and Coin Motifs).

*Chios, AR tetradrachm
ca. 420-350 BC*

KEOS: Coins from this small island of the Cyclades group, directly east of Cape Sunion, are very rare. As often is the case on island coins, a dolphin is included in the unimposing design. Keos was the home of the celebrated lyric poet Simonides, who was born about 50 years before this coin was struck.

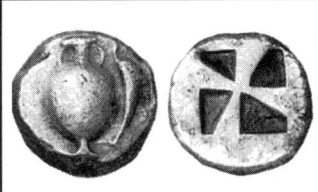

*Keos, Cyclades
AR stater
ca. 500-480 BC*

KOS: An island (and city) of the Sporades group off the coast of Caria and opposite Halikarnassos. The island was sacred to Asklepios and the site of the Asklepion, a famous temple built in honor of this god of healing. It was the home of the physician Hippocrates, as well as the poet Philetas and the painter Apelles.

*Kos, AR tetradrachm
ca. 300-190 BC*

NAXOS: This island is the largest of the Cyclades (not to be confused with the Sicilian city of the same name). Naxos was famous for its wine and figured prominently in the legends of Dionysos. It was here that the god found Ariadne, after she was left by Theseus. The didrachm illustrated here features a portrait of Dionysos along with a krater for the mixing of wine.

*Naxos, Cyclades
AR didrachm, ca. 190-160 BC*

49

PAROS: The island of Paros, birthplace of the eighth century poet Archilochos, is one of the larger of the Cyclades group, located south of Delos and about five miles west of Naxos. It was under Persian control until the defeat of Xerxes and then came into the Athenian sphere of influence. It was famous in antiquity for its superior marble which was used for fine sculpture.

Paros, Cyclades
AR drachm, ca. 490 BC

RHODOS: The easternmost island of the Aegean was settled by the Dorians and grew into a prosperous maritime confederacy with many colonies in Spain, Sicily, Italy and Asia Minor. The capital, Rhodos (Rhodes) was built in 408. Following the successful defense against a siege by Demetrios Poliorketes, the Rhodians sold the abandoned siege train. The proceeds were used to finance a colossal statue of Helios (one of the seven wonders of the ancient world) by the artist Chares. In 189 BC the Rhodian fleet aided Rome in its victory at Magnesia over Antiochos III of Syria. Under the Peace of Apamea, parts of Asia Minor were ceded to Rhodos—greatly improving its public wealth. In 167 the Romans declared Delos a free port, much to the detriment of Rhodos which had enjoyed unrestricted trade access and supremacy. The city's fortunes declined significantly from that point on.

Rhodos, AR tetradrachm
ca. 360 BC

SAMOS: This island off the coast of Ionia, in the Icarian Sea, was settled in Mycenaean times. The inhabitants were seafaring people and founded many colonies. The island was liberated from Persian control in the Battle of Mycale (479 BC) but was plagued with political problems for most of its history. The island of Samos was important for its production of wine, and was the home of the philosopher Pythagoras.

Samos, AR tetradrachm
ca. 370 BC

SALAMIS: This large land mass in the Saronic Gulf almost touches mainland Attica, and it is sometimes forgotten that it is an island. It is famous as the site of a naval victory in which the Persian fleet was defeated in 480 BC. Salamis was under Athenian control for most of its history and local issues are scarce.

*Salamis, AE 16 mm
ca. 400-330 BC*

TENEDOS: Only a small Aegean island, off the coast of Troas, Tenedos was mentioned by Homer. It was the spot to which the Greek fleet withdrew—making the Trojans think they had departed—while the Trojan Horse was being received into the city. After the Persian War the island became a tribute paying ally of Athens.

*Tenedos, AR tetradrachm
mid 2nd century BC*

THASOS: An island off the coast of Thrace in the Aegean Sea, was not only famous for its gold mines, but also as a center of cult worship to Dionysos. It was a fertile wine producing region, and also produced commercial pottery which often was stamped with designs from local coins. The island was at first under Phoenician control, then was colonized by settlers from Paros. It fell to the Persian general Mardonius, and subsequently to the Athenians. The fifth century was punctuated with conflicts between Thasos and Athens.

*Thasos, AR stater
ca. 430 BC*

There were numerous islands throughout the Mediterranean which struck coinage at one time or another, a few of them quite large and important, others barely large enough to sustain a settlement. It is amazing that some produced coinage at all. It may be that certain issues were struck more for the honor and prestige than for the practicality of use in commerce. This might account for the relative scarcity of some of these pieces—especially from the smaller islands.

Crete

The name of this large island south of the Peloponnesos is attributed to various sources, but the most likely is that it came from the first inhabitants who were called Curetes. According to legend, Minos, the son of Europa, expelled his brother Sarpedon and became ruler of the entire island and established a set of laws for its citizens. Cretan society was democratic from a very early period. The entire history and culture of the island is intertwined with the sea.

ITANOS: A fourth century stater from Itanos, on the eastern coast, depicts the sea deity Glaukos—a son of Poseidon endowed with the gift of prophesy.

Itanos, AR stater, ca. 380 BC

KNOSSOS: One of the most famous legends of Crete is that of the Minotaur, and the Labyrinth built by Daidalos at Knossos. It was here that Minos built his royal palace—the ruins of which may have actually inspired the myth. The Labyrinth is depicted on many coins of this city.

Knossos, AR tetradrachm, ca. 80 BC

LYTTOS was originally a Spartan colony, situated 80 stadia (about 10 miles) from the sea. The coin types from this city reflect the interests of a land based settlement, rather than sea creatures.

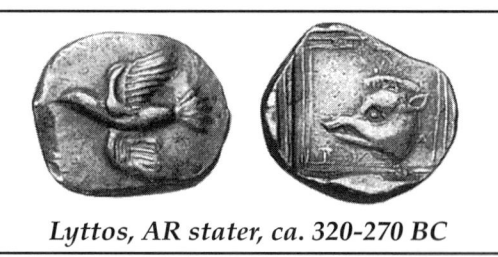
Lyttos, AR stater, ca. 320-270 BC

PHALASARNA: Coinage of this coastal city in the northwest of the island usually includes the trident of Poseidon as a city emblem. It possessed a commercial harbor.

Phalasarna, AR stater, ca. 280 BC

Cyprus

The island of Cyprus, south of the Anatolian coast, was famous in ancient times for its copper—from which it derives its name. It was colonized early by the Phoenicians, but in later times consisted of nine independent Greek states, each with their own king. It was a melting pot of cultural influences between East and West, but retained a special culture of its own. The goddess Aphrodite was worshipped throughout the island, especially at Paphos. After Alexander's conquest of the East, Cyprus fell under Ptolemaic control and was ruled at times by members of the royal family in residence.

SALAMIS was the most important of the Greek cities on Cyprus, and its Kings ruled the entire island at times. It was off the coast at Salamis that Demetrios Poliorketes met and defeated the fleet of Ptolemy in a famous naval battle. This victory was commemorated by the sculpture that we know as the "Nike of Samothrace" (Louvre, Paris).

KITION was one of the nine chief cities of Cyprus and possessed a good harbor. There was a salt works at this city that brought prosperity through trade. The celebrated Athenian general Kimon, who defeated the Persians at the river Eurymedon (468 BC), was in Cyprus due to the renewed war with Persia in 449. With 200 ships at his command, he fell ill and died at Kition.

Salamis, King Euagoras I AR tetrobol, ca 411-374 BC

Salamis, King Pnytagoras AV stater, 351-332 BC

Kition, King Pumiathon AV hemistater, 361-312 BC

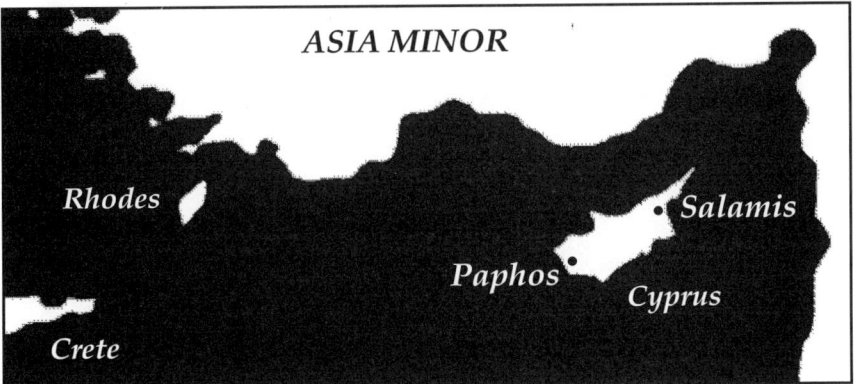

Mint Cities of Island Greeks

Amorgos, Aigiale
Amorgos, Arkesine
Amorgos, Minoa
Anaphe
Andros
Between Africa & Sicily, Cossura
Between Africa & Sicily, Gaulos
Between Africa & Sicily, Melita
Corcyra
Delos
Illyria, Issa
Illyria, Pharos, Herakleia
Illyria, Pharos
Ionia, Chios
Ionia, Samos
Ios
Ithaka
Keos, Darthaia
Keos, Iulis
Keos, Karthaia
Keos, Koressia
Kephallenia, Kranion
Kephallenia, Pale
Kephallenia, Pronnoi
Kephallenia, Same
Kythnos
Lemnos
Lemnos, Hephaistia
Lemnos, Myrina
Lesbos, Antissa
Lesbos, Eresos
Lesbos, Methymna
Lesbos, Mytilene
Lesbos, Nesos
Lesbos, Pordosilene

Lesbos, Pyrrha
Leukas
Melos
Mykonos
Mysia, Prokonnesos
Naxos
Off Caria, Astypalaia
Off Caria, Kalymna
Off Caria, Karpathos
Off Caria, Kos
Off Caria, Megiste
Off Caria, Nisyros
Off Caria, Syme
Off Caria, Telos
Off Lakonia, Kythera
Off Sicily, Lipara
Off Thessaly, Peparethos
Off Thessaly, Skiathos
Off Thessaly, Skyros
Off Thrace, Imbros
Off Thrace, Samothrake
Off Thrace, Thasos
Paros
Pholegandros
Rhodos, Ialysos
Rhodos, Kamiros
Rhodos, Lindos
Salamis
Seriphos
Sikinos
Siphnos
Syros
Tenos
Thera
Zakynthos

* Mint cities of Crete and Cyprus are included on the following page

Mint Cities of Crete	
Allaria	Latos
Anopolis	Lisos
Apollonia	Lyttos
Aptera	Malla
Arsinoe	Moda
Axos	Olonte
Biannos	Phaistos
Chersonasos	Phalasarna
Elyros	Polyrhenion
Gortyna	Praisos
Hierapytna	Priansos
Hyrtakina	Rhaukos
Itanos	Rhithymna
Keraia	Sybrita
Knosos	Tarrha
Kydonia	Tylisos
Lappa	

Mint Cities of Cyprus	
Amathus	Marion
Idalion	Paphos
Kition	Salamis
Lapethos	Soloi

BIBLIOGRAPHY

Island Greeks

Ashton, R. "Rhodian Coinage and the Colossus", *Revue Numismatique*, 1988.
Jackson, Anne E. "The Bronze Coinage of Gortyn", *Numismatic Chronicle*, 1971.
LeRider G. *Monnaies Crétoises du V^Eau IER Siècle av. J.-C.*, Paris, 1966.
Metropolitan Museum of Art. *Greek Art of the Aegean Islands*, (art exhibition—no coins but valuable text, New York, 1980.
Price, Martin. "A Hoard From Gortyn", *Revue Numismatique*, 1966.
Svoronos, J. *Numismatique de la Crète Ancienne*, Paris, 1890.

Black Sea Area

APOLLONIA PONTICA: As one might suspect from the name, Apollo was the patron of this Thracian town on the Black Sea. It was the site of a temple and famous colossal statue of the god, who appears on this tetradrachm. The anchor seems to have been a heraldic badge of this city as it graces many of the coins issued there.

Apollonia Pontika
AR tetradrachm, ca. 400 BC

KROMNA: Gem-like silver tetrobols bearing the head of Zeus on the obverse and that of Hera on the reverse were struck at Kromna, in Paphlagonia, from 340 to 300 BC. The series ended when its inhabitants were relocated to the newly

Kromna, AR tetrobol
ca. 340-300 BC

founded Bithynian city of Amastris. The delicacy of style in this issue demonstrates that even some of the smaller, more remote, cities were able to acquire the services of a master celator.

PANTIKAPAION: This city was an important sea port and trading center on the Cimmerian Bosporos in the Tauric Chersonese (northeastern region of the Black Sea). It was founded by the Milesians about 541 BC and was the residence of the Kings of the Bosporos. Many great treasures of gold metalwork have been found archaeologically in this region, mostly in Skythian tombs. Whether this art was produced in the Bosporos or imported from Northern Greece is uncertain, but the local production of magnificent coins leaves open the possibility that a center of artistic achievement blossomed in the fourth century.

Pantikapaion, AV stater (Pan)
ca. 350 BC

Pantikapaion, AE 17mm
(Pan/Bull) ca. 3rd century BC

SINOPE: Located on the north coast of Asia Minor, Sinope was settled by Milesians in the eighth century. It was repopulated in 632 by the Milesians after being destroyed during the Cimmerian invasion and subsequently became the most important commercial center on the Euxine. The city was the birthplace and residence of Mithradates the Great. The coins of this city usually portray a sea eagle, sometimes carrying a dolphin in its talons. The nymph Sinope is also included on several types.

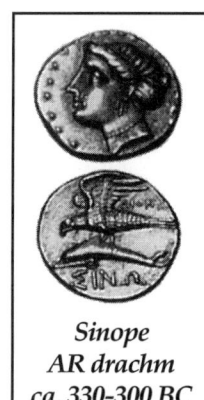

Sinope
AR drachm
ca. 330-300 BC

ISTROS solved the problem of having to turn a coin around to look at it. On a silver drachm issued in the fourth century, this Black Sea settlement placed two heads side by side in opposite directions. Speculation about the meaning of this motif ranges from the Dioscouri to a personification of the Danube—which the ancients thought flowed both north and south.

Istros, AR drachm
ca. 4th century BC

OLBIA was a Milesian colony located between two rivers on the northernmost point of the Black Sea. The city prospered from trade and was especially important in the third to first centuries. An interesting series of cast coinage in unusual shapes and sizes was issued at Olbia. Large cast bronze coins of about 70 millimeters in diameter and 115 grams in weight were produced with facing heads on the obverse (Demeter is depicted here) and on the reverse, a flying eagle with a dolphin in its talons. It is hard to believe that these massive coins served any useful purpose in commerce, due to their impractical size and weight.

Olbia, AE 68mm (actual size)
ca. 400-350 BC

KOLCHIS: Although considered a country of Asia, because of its location on the east coast of the Black Sea, Kolchis figures prominently in Greek mythology and trade relations. It is mentioned by Aeschylus and Pindar, and is the place where Jason and the Argonauts supposedly found the "Golden Fleece". The main city, Dioskourias, traded actively with Milesian settlements on the northern coast of Asia Minor. Native princes of Kolchis were independent until they were subdued by Mithradates the Great in the first century BC and became part of the Pontic Kingdom.

Kolchis, AR hemidrachm, ca. 5th century BC

Mint Cities of the Black Sea

Abonuteichos, Paphlagonia	Mesembria
Amastris, Paphlagonia	Odessos
Amisos, Pontos	Olbia
Apollonia Pontika	Pantikapaion
Chersonesos	Phanagoreia
Dia, Bithynia	Pharnakia, Pontos
Dioskourias, Kolchis	Sesamos, Paphlagonia
Gorgippia	Sinope, Paphlagonia
Herakleia Pontika, Bithynia	Tion, Bithynia
Istros	Tomis
Kallatis	Trapezus, Pontos
Kromna, Paphlagonia	Tyra

BIBLIOGRAPHY
Black Sea Area

British Museum. *Sylloge Nummorum Graecorum, Vol. IX, The British Museum, Part 1, The Black Sea,* London, 1993.
Dittrich, K. *Ancient Coins from Olbia and Panticapaeum,* London, N.D.
Hind, J.G.F. "Istrian Faces and the River Danube", *Numismatic Chronicle,* 1970.
Malloy, A. G. *The Coinage of Amisus,* New York, 1970.
Minns, E.H. *Scythians and Greeks,* Neudruck, New York, 1971.
Shelov, D.B. *Coinage of the Bosporus,* (BAR) Int. Series 46, 1978.
Vagi, David L. "4th century drachms of Sinope", *The Celator,* 2 parts, Vol. 8, Nos. 6&7, June/July 1994.
Zograph, A.N. *Ancient Coinage,* BAR Supp. Series 33 (1977).

The Black Sea "Hoard"

In December, 1988, a group of debased silver diobols, of the types found at the Black Sea settlements of Mesembria and Apollonia Pontika, appeared in the ancient coin market. They were quickly condemned in the trade, as well as by the curator of Greek coins at the British Museum. Consequently, the original purchaser commissioned an independent analyst to do a metallurgical study. Electron scanning microscope tests indicated that the coins were ancient. A bitter and prolonged controversy developed, pitting the tools of modern science against the "street smart" experience of professional numismatists. The controversy raged for five years and was a frequent topic in the numismatic press.

Finally, an American dealer visiting Bulgaria found that some of these coins were being sold—as replicas—at the National Museum in Sofia. Subsequently, modern dies used to make these replicas were offered for sale in New York, and huge bags of the fakes were offered to dealers at a few dollars each. The dies and the replicas die-matched with coins in the analysis. The diobols were subsequently condemned as "ancient counterfeits" in the *Bulletin on Counterfeits* issued by the International Bureau for the Suppression of Counterfeit Coins. This basically ended the debate.

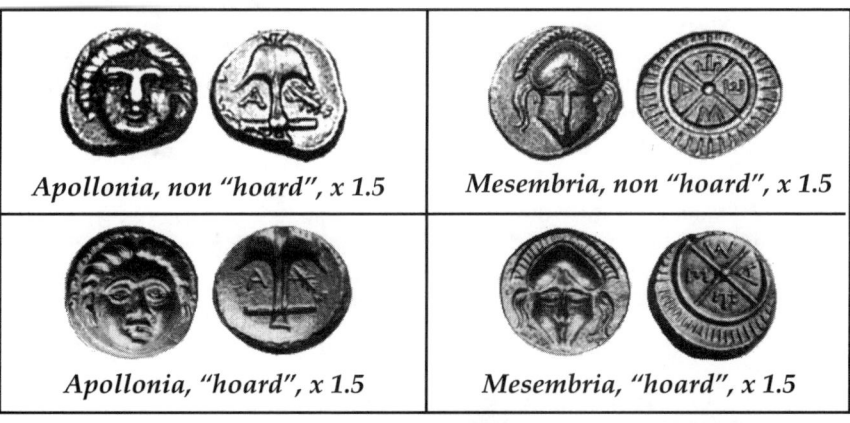

Apollonia, non "hoard", x 1.5 *Mesembria, non "hoard", x 1.5*

Apollonia, "hoard", x 1.5 *Mesembria, "hoard", x 1.5*

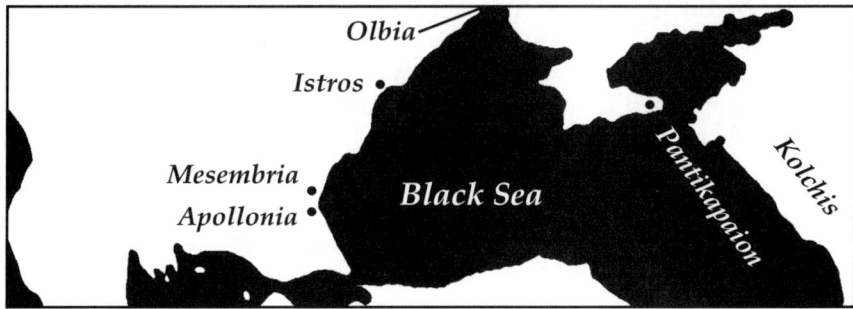

Asia Minor

In the centuries following the collapse of the Mycenaean civilization, the coastal areas of Asia Minor were settled by three groups of people. The Dorians, from the north, settled in southwest Asia Minor, the Ionians settled the central-western coast and islands, and the Aeolians settled the northwest coastal areas. Scattered in small settlements, these people tended to associate themselves with others for mutual aid. The Greeks were a fiercely independent people, but as major powers developed there came into existence a sort of colonial system which allied various smaller cities with a "mother city".

Shortly after the invention of coinage, which is commonly believed to have originated in Lydia or Ionia during the 7th century, Persian expeditions into Asia Minor secured their dominance in the region. A system of satrapal governors was installed and despite continuing growth and prosperity many of the Greek cities of Asia Minor remained under Persian control until the army of Alexander crossed into Asia.

LYDIA: During his reign, Croesus (Kroisos in Greek) expanded the Kingdom of Lydia deep into Asia Minor. He was a talented leader of a prosperous region. The coinage of Croesus is popular, not only for its historical interest, but also because of the role that Croesus played in the development of monetary systems. His coins were the first to be struck in denominations of both gold and silver. More importantly, they had a fixed relationship of 13:1. The denominations in gold ranged from the stater to 1/12 stater, and in silver from the stater to 1/24 stater. They were perfectly interchangeable.

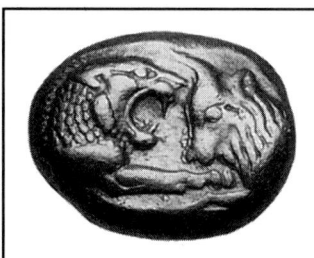
Croesus, AR stater. (x2)
ca. 561-546 BC

EPHESOS: This Ionian settlement at the mouth of the Cayster river became the main seaport and center of trade serving the Maeander river valley. The bee which appears as a heraldic symbol on coinage of Ephesos is usually coupled with a stag. Both images symbolize the cult worship of Artemis, whose temple at that city was a famous edifice.

Ephesos, AR tetradrachm
ca. 387-295 BC

LAMPSAKOS: An important city on the Hellespont, Lampsakos was the chief seat of the worship of Priapos (the son of Dionysos and Aphrodite). The city must have enjoyed a flourishing culture, as coins struck at Lampsakos are exceptional more often than not. The gold stater illustrated here is a rare masterpiece of Hellenistic art.

Lampsakos, AV stater ca. 360 BC (Helios)

PERGAMON: One of the most famous cities of Asia Minor, this was the site of the Pergamene Altar to Zeus. Its great library was appropriated by Mark Antony and given to Cleopatra to replace the one at Alexandria which burned.

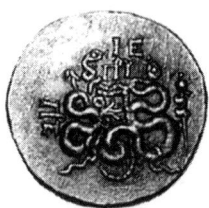

Pergamon, AR cistophoric tetradrachm after 133 BC
(snake crawling from cista [basket])

SIDE: This coastal Pamphylian city was founded by Aiolians from Kyme. It was built near the mouth of the Melas (Apple) river—which accounts for the pomegranate, the ancient "apple of the gods", found on some coins struck there.

Side, AR tetradrachm, ca. 190-150 BC
(pomegranate in reverse field)

TARSOS: A city of great antiquity, and chief city of Cilicia, Tarsos was located on the banks of the river Kydnos. In ancient times, it had an approach to the sea. It was settled by the Greeks at an early date, but was mainly in Persian hands until the arrival of Alexander.

Tarsos, AR stater, 361-334 BC
(Baaltars holding eagle)

Stephanophoroi of Aiolis and Ionia

During the second century BC, as a result of Rome's success against the Hellenistic monarchies, a cluster of cities in western Asia Minor enjoyed a new sense of freedom. In response, these cities (historically unimposing for the most part) struck autonomous tetradrachms of a uniform style and purpose. The weights of these coins conform to the Attic standard and are identical in weight to the "New Style" Athens tetradrachms. They were obviously intended—perhaps wishfully in some cases—to trade in the same environment. Like those from Athens, these too bear a reverse motif set within an encircling wreath (Stephanophoroi = wreath bearers). Although the coinage was not produced over a particularly long period of time, the inevitable hoard finds associated with a trade coin make most of these pieces relatively inexpensive for such large and attractive types.

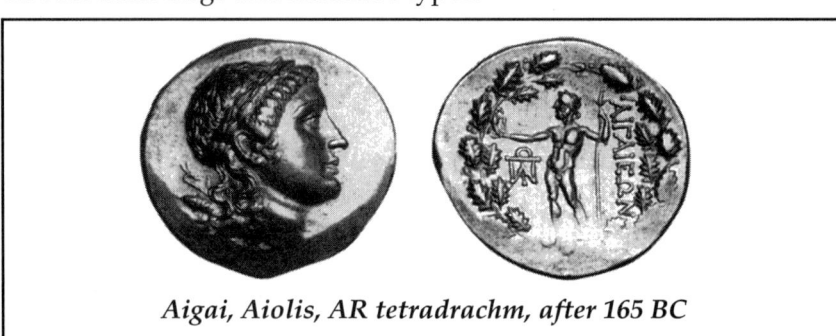

Aigai, Aiolis, AR tetradrachm, after 165 BC

AIGAI was an inland city on the Pythikos (or Hyllos?) River, southeast of Myrina and north of Smyrna. Little is recorded of the history of this place, but it must have been a city of some importance to issue such impressive tetradrachms. The obverse features Apollo laureate and on the reverse is Zeus holding an eagle and scepter. These coins are scarce, and probably did not circulate as widely as those from more prominent cities.

Kyme, Aiolis, AR tetradrachm, after 165 BC

KYME was the largest of the Aiolian cities, situated on a bay into which flowed the rivers Kaikos and Hermos. According to legend, it was founded by the Amazon Kyme. The Amazons were a mythical tribe of warlike women from Pontos (or variously from Kolchis, Thrace or Skythia), who fought against Greek heroes. A battle, referred to as the "Amazonomachy", provided poets and artists with wonderful material for narration. The head of Kyme wearing a taenia in her hair is presented on this tetradrachm's obverse, while the reverse features a horse prancing—probably in allusion to the prosperous equine industry of this region.

Myrina, Aiolis, AR tetradrachm, after 165 BC

MYRINA, a fortified city and apparently one of greater importance than history has suggested, honored Apollo on its tetradrachms. The nearby Temple of Apollo at Grynion was a tourist attraction of some renown, and probably important to the commerce of the city. Myrina was also known for its fine terra-cottas. On this tetradrachm we find a sensitive portrait of Apollo Grynios, backed by a view of Apollo holding a branch and phiale while walking to the right.

Herakleia ad Latmon, Ionia, AR tetradrachm, after 165 BC

HERAKLEIA AD LATMON was sited on the shore of a gulf at the foot of Mt. Latmos in Ionia. Aside from the fact that a nearby cave was respected as the tomb of Endymion, little is known about this place. It did not issue coinage earlier than the Hellenistic period. The tetradrachms feature a helmeted Athena on obverse and club on reverse.

Lebedos, Ionia, AR tetradrachm, ca. 150 BC

LEBEDOS stood on the coast between Colophon and Teos. The city was greatly depopulated by Lysimachos in the first quarter of the third century, and after that was regarded as a desolate place. It did, however, maintain enough prestige to produce this attractive tetradrachm which complements the series issued by its neighbors. The type is a thinly veiled imitation (or flattery) of the Athenian tetradrachms. On the obverse we find the helmeted head of Athena, and on the reverse an owl standing on a club set between cornucopias. Like the types from Aigai and Herakleia ad Latmon, this issue is relatively scarce.

Magnesia, Ionia, AR tetradrachm, ca. 160-150 BC

MAGNESIA, on the Lethaios river (a tributary of the Maeander), was located southeast of Ephesos. It is sometimes called Magnesia ad Maeandrum. The city was originally founded by Thessalians, but was destroyed about 700 BC during a Cimmerian invasion. It was repopulated by Miletians and became a prosperous settlement. Magnesia was one of the cities given to Themistokles by Artaxerxes. It was the site of an important temple, built by the architect Hermogenes and dedicated to Artemis Leucophryene. On the Hellenistic tetradrachms of Magnesia, Artemis wears a stephane in her hair and carries the bow and quiver, which are standard attributes of this goddess, across her back. The reverse of these coins depicts Apollo, the brother of Artemis, standing above a maeander pattern.

Smyrna, Ionia, AR tetradrachm, after 165 BC

SMYRNA was originally settled by Aiolians or Ionians, but was taken and destroyed by Alyattes of Lydia. It was repopulated by Antigonos of Macedon late in the fourth century and became one of the most important cultural centers in Asia Minor. Due to its deep and safe natural harbor, it is the only one of the cities included in this section which survives today. It also enjoyed the proximity of a fertile river valley and fresh mountain water. Smyrna provided a link between Sardeis and the sea, and became a great emporium for trade. The city boasted of being the birthplace of Homer, but was not alone in this claim. The tetradrachm struck during the second century have on their obverse a turreted head of Kybele and on the reverse a wreath bearing the ethnic.

BIBLIOGRAPHY
Asia Minor

Jones, Nicholas F. "The Autonomous Wreathed Tetradrachms of Magnesia-on-Maeander", *ANS Museum Notes* 24 (1979).

Kleiner, Fred S. and Sidney P. Noe. *The Early Cistophoric Coinage,* ANS Numismatic Studies 14, New York, 1977.

Levante, Edoardo. *Sylloge Nummorum Graecorum, Switzerland; E. Levante - Cilicia,* Bern, 1986 (supplement I, Zürich, 1993).

Lindgren H. and F. Kovacs. *Ancient Bronze Coinage of Asia Minor and the Levant,* San Mateo, 1985.

Milne, J.G. "The Silver Coinage of Smyrna", *Numismatic Chronicle,* 1914.

Oakley, John H. "The Autonomous Wreathed Tetradrachms of Kyme, Aeolis", *ANS Museum Notes* 27 (1982).

Sacks, Kenneth S. "The Wreathed Coins of Aeolian Myrina". *ANS Museum Notes* 30 (1985).

Von Aulock, Hans. *Sylloge Nummorum Graecorum, Sammlung Hans von Aulock,* Berlin, 1957-1968 (1987 reprint in four volumes).

Waddington, W.H. *Recueil général des monnaies grecques d'Asie Mineure,* Paris, 1904-1912.

Mint Cities of Asia Minor

Aiolis, Boione
Aiolis, Elaia
Aiolis, Grynion
Aiolis, Kyme
Aiolis, Larissa Phrikonis
Aiolis, Myrina
Aiolis, Neonteichos
Aiolis, Temnos
Aiolis, Tisna
Aiolis, Aigai
Aiolis, Autokane
Bithynia, Apameia (Myrleia)
Bithynia, Astakos
Bithynia, Bithynion
Bithynia, Kalchedon
Bithynia, Kalchedon
Bithynia, Kios
Bithynia, Nikaia
Bithynia, Nikomedia
Cappadocia, Eusebeia (Mazaca)
Caria, Alabanda
Caria, Alinda
Caria, Amyzon
Caria, Antiocheia
Caria, Antiocheia Ad Maeandrum
Caria, Aphrodisias-Plarasa
Caria, Apollonia Salbake
Caria, Astyra
Caria, Attuda
Caria, Bargylia
Caria, Chalketor
Caria, Euhippe
Caria, Euromos
Caria, Gordioteichos
Caria, Halikarnassos
Caria, Harpasa
Caria, Herakleia Salbake
Caria, Hydisos
Caria, Iasos
Caria, Idyma
Caria, Karpathos
Caria, Karyanda
Caria, Kaunos
Caria, Keramos
Caria, Kidramos
Caria, Knidos
Caria, Mylasa
Caria, Myndos
Caria, Neapolis
Caria, Orthosia
Caria, Stratonikeia
Caria, Tabai
Caria, Termera
Cilicia, Adana
Cilicia, Aigai
Cilicia, Alexandria Ad Issum
Cilicia, Anazarbos
Cilicia, Antiocheia
Cilicia, Aphrodisias
Cilicia, Elaiussa
Cilicia, Hieropolis-Kastabala
Cilicia, Holmi
Cilicia, Issos
Cilicia, Kelenderis
Cilicia, Kibyra Minor
Cilicia, Korykos
Cilicia, Mallos
Cilicia, Mopsos
Cilicia, Nagidos
Cilicia, Seleukeia
Cilicia, Soloi
Cilicia, Tarsos
Cilicia, Zephyrion
Galatia, Pessinus
Galatia, Tavion
Ionia, Arsinoeia
Ionia, Ephesos
Ionia, Erythrai

Note: Black Sea coastal cities of Asia Minor are included in the previous section entitled Black Sea Area

Asia Minor cont.

Ionia, Eurydikeia
Ionia, Herakleia Ad Latmon
Ionia, Klazomenai
Ionia, Kolophon
Ionia, Larissa
Ionia, Lebedos
Ionia, Leukai
Ionia, Magnesia
Ionia, Metropolis
Ionia, Miletos
Ionia, Myus
Ionia, Naulochos
Ionia, Oinoe
Ionia, Phokaia
Ionia, Phygela
Ionia, Priene
Ionia, Smyrna
Ionia, Teos
Lycaonia, Eikonion
Lycaonia, Parlais
Lycia, Antiphellos
Lycia, Aperlai
Lycia, Apollonia
Lycia, Arykanda
Lycia, Balbura
Lycia, Bubon
Lycia, Choma
Lycia, Gagai
Lycia, Kalynda
Lycia, Kragos
Lycia, Kyaneai
Lycia, Limyra
Lycia, Masikytes
Lycia, Myra
Lycia, Nisa
Lycia, Oinoanda
Lycia, Olympos
Lycia, Patara
Lycia, Phaselis
Lycia, Phaselis
Lycia, Phellos
Lycia, Pinara
Lycia, Rhodiapolis
Lycia, Telmessos
Lycia, Termessos Minor
Lycia, Tlos
Lycia, Trebenna
Lycia, Tybenissos
Lycia, Xanthos
Lydia, Aninetos
Lydia, Apollonis
Lydia, Blaundos
Lydia, Kaystrianoi, The
Lydia, Klannudda
Lydia, Magnesia Ad Sipylum
Lydia, Mostene
Lydia, Nysa
Lydia, Philadelpheia
Lydia, Sardeis
Lydia, Stratonikeia
Lydia, Thyateira
Lydia, Tralleis
Mysia, Adramytteion
Mysia, Apollonia Ad Rhyndakon
Mysia, Atarneus
Mysia, Gambrion
Mysia, Kisthene
Mysia, Kyzikos
Mysia, Lampsakos
Mysia, Miletopolis
Mysia, Parion
Mysia, Pergamon
Mysia, Perperene
Mysia, Pitane
Mysia, Plakia
Mysia, Poimanenon
Mysia, Priapos
Mysia, Teuthrania
Mysia, Thebe
Mysia, Zeleia
Pamphylia, Aspendos
Pamphylia, Attaleia

Asia Minor cont.

Pamphylia, Perge
Pamphylia, Side
Pamphylia, Sillyon
Paphlagonia, Pimolisa
Paphlagonia, Pompieopolis
Phrygia, Abbaitis
Phrygia, Aizanis
Phrygia, Akmoneia
Phrygia, Amorion
Phrygia, Apameia
Phrygia, Appia
Phrygia, Dionysopolis
Phrygia, Eriza
Phrygia, Eumeneia
Phrygia, Hierapolis
Phrygia, Hydrela
Phrygia, Kibyra
Phrygia, Kolossai
Phrygia, Laodikeia
Phrygia, Leonnaia
Phrygia, Peltai
Phrygia, Philomelion
Phrygia, Prymnessos
Phrygia, Sanaus
Phrygia, Synnada
Pisidia, Adada
Pisidia, Etenna
Pisidia, Isinda
Pisidia, Keraitai
Pisidia, Komama
Pisidia, Kremna
Pisidia, Sagalassos
Pisidia, Selge
Pisidia, Termessos Major
Pontos, Amaseia
Pontos, Chabakta
Pontos, Gaziura
Pontos, Kabeira
Pontos, Komana
Pontos, Laodikeia
Pontos, Taulara
Troas, Abydos
Troas, Achilleion
Troas, Alexandreia Troas
Troas, Antandros
Troas, Antiocheia
Troas, Assos
Troas, Birytis
Troas, Dardanos
Troas, Gargara
Troas, Gentinos
Troas, Gergis
Troas, Hamaxitos
Troas, Ilion
Troas, Kebren
Troas, Kolone
Troas, Lamponeia
Troas, Neandreia
Troas, Ophrynion
Troas, Rhoeteion
Troas, Sigeion
Troas, Skamandria
Troas, Skepsis
Troas, Tenedos
Troas, Thymbra

The East

Most of the coins struck in the regions east of Asia Minor were the product of cultures other than Greek. These include Persian and Armenian coins, which have been classified for our purposes as coins of "Non-Classical Cultures". They will be dealt with in a later volume of this series. The coins of Phoenicia are mentioned here, because many of the "Greek" cities that we mention in other regions were originally founded by the Phoenicians. Although not technically Greek until after the conquest of Alexander, the coinage of these cities is closely related.

The Greek coinage in Baktria, struck by Alexander's successors, is essentially portrait coinage. These types are covered in the later section on Hellenistic portrait coins. There are also bronze coins from the region which are not portrait bearing. They usually depict Greek deities.

The Seleukid Kingdom extended, at one time or another, into most of the lands between Syria and Baktria. Their coinage is also published in the portrait section. Bibliographic references in that section will provide information on the non-portrait coins as well.

Another Greek kingdom in the southeastern corner of Anatolia is known as the Kings of Commagene. These were descendants of the Seleukid family, and they managed to carve out a small protected area which survived into the first century AD.

Historical information is sketchy in most of these regions. For more detailed information about the Eastern cities we highly recommend David Sear's *Greek Coins and Their Values,* Vol. II. For the beginning collector, this is an indispensable guide to coin issuing cities and a reference book that every collector of Greek coins should acquire.

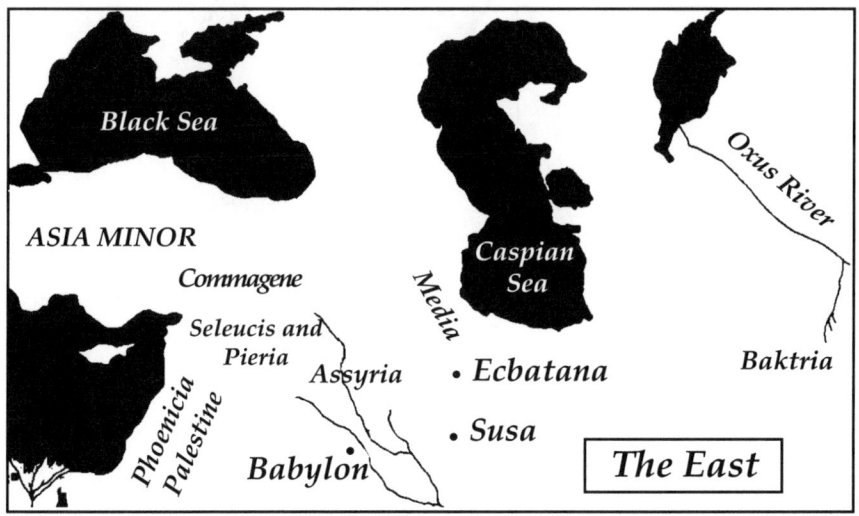

Phoenicia

Phoenicia has a long and interesting history of interaction with the Greek people, and was occupied at various times by the Seleukids of Syria and the Ptolemies of Egypt. The early coinage is especially appealing to the collector who enjoys research, since much of it is undocumented. This is one series where new discoveries are still possible.

Bodashtart, King of Sidon, AR tetrashekel, ca. 384-370 BC

The tetrashekel from Sidon illustrated here is one such example. The history of these kings of Phoenicia is obscure. Coins bearing similar motifs were issued in a variety of denominations, including gold.

Tyre, AR shekel, 111/110 BC

Among collectors, one of the most popular coins from Phoenicia is the "Shekel of Tyre". This silver trade coin, of tetradrachm proportions, circulated in the region for a very long time without

Arados, AR tetradrachm, 95/94 BC

any significant changes in style. It is traditionally regarded as the type comprising the infamous 30 pieces of silver exchanged for the betrayal of Christ.

Another Phoenician city that produced interesting coin types was Arados. Although the city was actually located on an island, Arados controlled significant resources on the mainland. In addition to the conservative tetradrachm, with a turreted Tyche (goddess of good fortune), the city produced a large issue of bronze coins bearing sea gods or myths. They also issued a lengthy series of silver drachms of the type seen at Ephesos with bee and stag. It has been suggested that this was prompted by a monetary alliance, or at least some trade consideration.

Mint Cities of The East

Arachosia, Kapisa
Assyria, Atusia
Assyria, Demetrias
Baktria, Baktra
Baktria, (Aï Khanoum)
Coele-syria, Chalkis
Coele-syria, Damaskos
Coele-syria, Demetrias
Commagene, Samosata
Cyrrhestica, Bambyce
Mesopotamia, Babylon
Mesopotamia, Seleukeia
Palestine, Askalon
Palestine, Gaza
Persia, Ecbatana
Phoenicia, Arados
Phoenicia, Berytos
Phoenicia, Byblos (Gebal)
Phoenicia, Dora
Phoenicia, Karne
Phoenicia, Marathos
Phoenicia, Orthosia
Phoenicia, Ptolemais-Ake
Phoenicia, Sidon
Phoenicia, Tripolis
Phoenicia, Tyre
Seleukis And Pieria, Antiocheia
Seleukis And Pieria, Apameia
Seleukis And Pieria, Epiphaneia
Seleukis And Pieria, Gabala
Seleukis And Pieria, Laodikeia
Seleukis And Pieria, Larissa
Seleukis And Pieria, Rhosos
Seleukis And Pieria, Seleukeia
Susiana, Susa

BIBLIOGRAPHY
The East

Bellinger, Alfred. "The Coins from the Treasure of the Oxus", *ANS Museum Notes* X, 1962.
Bopearachchi, Osmund. *Monnaies Gréco-Bactriennes et Indo-Grecques,* Paris, 1991.
Bopearachchi, O. and A. ur Rahman. *Pre-Kushana Coins in Pakistan,* Karachi, 1995.
Gardner, P. *The Coins of the Greek and Scythic Kings of Bactria and India,* London, 1886.
Mitchiner, Michael A. *Oriental Coins and Their Values: The Ancient and Classical World 600 B.C - A.D. 600,* London, 1978.
_____. *Indo-Greek and Indo-Scythian Coinage,* 9 vols., London, 1975-76.
Tarn, W.W. *The Greeks in Bactria and India,* 2nd ed. Cambridge, 1951.
Whitehead, R.B. *Indo-Greek Numismatics,* (compilation of *Numismatic Chronicle* articles from 1923 to 1950), Argonaut, Chicago 1969.
_____. *Catalogue of Coins in the Panjab Museum, Vol. I, Indo-Greek Coins,* Lahore, 1914 (Argonaut reprint, 1969).

North Africa

CARTHAGE: This famous city, in the region called Zeugitana, was founded by Tyrian colonists from Phoenicia in the eighth century BC. It became a great maritime trading center and dominated the western Mediterranean. In the second century BC the population was said to be 700,000. Depictions of

Carthage, AV trihemistater ca. 260 BC

the deities Tanit/Artemis, and Herakles/Melqarth, are common on the coinage of Carthage—as are reverse depictions of lions, horses and palm trees. The Carthaginians invaded Sicily in 480 and again in 410 BC, and struck an extensive series of coinage during their occupation of the western part of the island. It is commonly referred to as Siculo-Punic, and is an appealing blend of styles. Clashes with the Romans led to a series of three wars, known as the Punic Wars, which ultimately left Carthage in ruins.

KYRENE: The coastal city of Kyrene was founded by Greeks from the island of Thera. It was advantageously situated between Carthage and Egypt, and directly south of the Peloponnesos. The city achieved great wealth through trade in Silphium. This plant, which by Roman times became extinct, was famous and highly sought after for medicinal purposes. Many of the coins struck at Kyrene bear depictions of the Silphium plant.

Kyrene, AR tetradrachm ca. 460 BC.

BARKE: This inland city was founded about 560 BC by Greek settlers from Kyrene. It became quite powerful, and virtually independent of its mother city. The Persians took Barke in 510 and relocated most of the inhabitants to Baktria, where a town of the same name was established.

Barke, Kyrenaica AR tetradrachm, ca. 400 BC

NUMIDIA: Juba I was a notorious ruler who sided with Pompey in the Roman Civil War and lost. He committed suicide in 46 BC following Caesar's victory. The bronze coin illustrated here bears a personification of Numidia wearing an elephant-skin headdress.

Juba I, Numidia, AE 22mm, 60-46 BC

Mint Cities of North Africa	
Byzacium, Alipota (Sullecti)	Mauretania, Tingis
Byzacium, Hadrumetum	Mauretania, Zilis
Byzacium, Thaena	Numidia, Bulla Regia
Byzacium, Thysdrus	Numidia, Cirta
Kyrenaica, Barke	Numidia, Gadiauphala
Kyrenaica, Euesperides	Numidia, Hippo Regius and Tipasa
Kyrenaica, Kyrene	Numidia, Macomades
Kyrenaica, Ptolemais	Numidia, Salviana
Kyrenaica, Teuchira	Numidia, Suthul
Mauretania, Camarata	Numidia, Thabraca and Tuniza
Mauretania, Lix	Numidia, Thagura
Mauretania, Rusadir	Numidia, Zarai
Mauretania, Sala	Syrtica, Leptis Magna
Mauretania, Semes	Syrtica, Oea
Mauretania, Tamusia	Syrtica, Sabratha
Mauretania, Timici	Zeugitana, Carthage

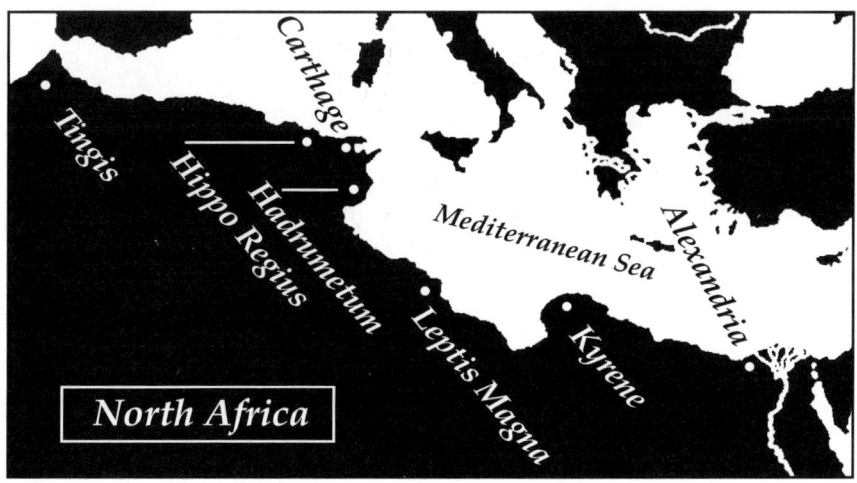

73

Artistry of the Celator

In Plato's classification of occupations, celature (the art of engraving in bas-relief) ranks very high. Although we do not know a great deal about the artists who worked in this medium, enough fragments of information exist to suggest that in their own time skilled celators were eagerly sought and amply rewarded. The most important cities and rulers retained one or more master celators on a permanent basis. Others were relegated to hiring expertise as the need and opportunity arose.

It is clear that celators travelled between cities to produce dies for various local mints. In some cases we find the signature of an important celator inscribed into the dies of more than one city. In other cases, the signature of the artist is found in the virtuosity of his own hand, which allows us to recognize his work. It also seems that artists of superior skill regularly took on apprentices, which led to schools of design and techniques that are often identifiable. There are many Greek coin types which exhibit a wide divergence in the quality of workmanship from one specimen to the next. From this it seems clear that in at least some of these cases a master craftsman was employed to create the prototype and perhaps an initial supply of dies. As these dies were consumed they were replaced by inferior copies made locally.

Celators did not work in an isolated medium. One can see distinct relationships between conventions of representation on coins and those on painted vases, metalwork, jewelry and in sculpture. Heraldic devices often appear in several media, as do such conventions as chariots at the turnpole or distinctive portrayal of mythological creatures. Numismatic art may have been a more conservative medium than some of the others, but experimentation with perspective, narration, motion and other avant garde devices is not unknown.

At Delphi, in the first half of the 5th century, a silver tridrachm was struck with a design consisting of two rams' heads back to back. While visually intriguing, the image is actually a depiction of two Persian rhyta (drinking cups). These ornate cups were produced in precious metals, and were unknown in Greece prior to the Persian War. Herodotus relates that the rhyta were among the spoils of the Battle of Plataea. Some were undoubtedly deposited at Delphi as a sacrifice. Shortly thereafter, cop-

Delphi, AR tridrachm, after 479 BC

ies were produced by Attic potters, and here we see the rhyta as a coin motif—perhaps alluding to temple deposits, but certainly an attractive design in itself.

Stylistic changes were usually reflected in all art media within a very short time. The facing gorgon head provides a typical example of how sculptors, potters and celators shared in their approach. The convention of facing heads is a much touted numismatic theme, with spectacular examples appearing in the 5th century and later. As an artistic convention, however, its origin is much earlier. The rigid frontality of archaic sculpture provided a foundation for the technique which enjoyed so much success in later periods. The facing gorgon head may be seen in sculptural relief from the late 7th century, and in Attic vases of the 7th and 6th centuries. It appeared on the coinage of Athens in the middle of the 6th century. The gorgon is perhaps an exception since it always appears facing, but the fact that artists understood the dynamics of a facing presentation at such an early stage is significant.

Sculptural relief - 7th C. BC

Attic pottery - 6th C. BC

One of the aesthetic problems that celators struggled with is the effective utilization of a circular space. On reverse dies, this issue was sometimes avoided by framing the design in a square which left an incuse punch mark. This also served to push extra metal into high relief obverse designs.

In some cases, the artist attempted merely to transfer an image or theme from another medium. This seldom produced acceptable results. The slavish copying of a narrative scene from the panel of a painted vase or sculptural frieze rarely achieved the desired effect on a coin planchet since the boundaries of the media are so dissimilar. From a very early period in the evolution of numismatic art this problem was recognized and dealt with in various ways and with varying degrees of success. The facing head of a gorgon, on the Attic tetradrachm of 530 BC, lent itself well to this circular space and the celator used that to his advantage. In this case, the result was even more effective than that of the contemporary tondo design illustrated just above (tondo is the term used

Attic tetradrachm, ca. 530 BC.

by modern art historians to describe the center decoration of a Kylix or wide bodied cup used for drinking wine).

Not all celators were so accomplished, nor were all motifs so adaptable. In some cases the artist was undoubtedly relegated to dealing with a theme of someone else's choosing. Illustrated below are examples of failure and success in the application of motif to medium. Although struck on a large planchet, the rectangular motif of the Derrones dodekadrachm creates technical as well as aesthetic problems with the corners clipped and no sense of balance. The Syracusan artist took a similar rectangular motif and adapted it to the circular space by causing the charioteer to lean forward as he goads the horse to his left—whose head is raised in response. Interposed between the head of the driver and that of the background horse is Nike floating through the air as she crowns the victorious team. Her wings gracefully conform to the border of dots and provide visual continuity for the adaptation. Below the baseline a sea monster glides effortlessly with its head and tail raised as its body rounds out the scene. The result is the pleasing transformation

Derrones, AR dodekadrachm ca. 485 BC

Syracuse AR tetradrachm ca. 460 BC

of a rectangular motif, probably designed originally for the panel of an amphora or other painted vase, into something appropriate on coinage. The examples illustrated here were chosen because of their proximity in dates—later Syracusan coinage exhibits even further refinement of this principle as motion and emotion evolve in numismatic art.

The way that artists portrayed their subject was then, as it is today, a reflection of contemporary taste. That is, it reflected certain styles. The collector will sometimes find references in sale catalogues to a coin of "the finest style". This is a totally inappropriate description, since style cannot be measured qualitatively. What the cataloguer perhaps could say is that a coin is struck in a pleasing style, a realistic style, or a style with great sensitivity and emotion. Not, however, a good, better or best style. Classical art is not rendered in a better style than Archaic art, it is rendered in a style that more accurately depicts the physical world. Is this better? Not necessarily. As Thomas Aquinas said, "Beauty is what pleases the eye". Some would argue that French Impressionism is more beautiful than reality, because in it the mind sees its own beauty. Without going into a treatise on style, we should say simply that the art of the ancients is as varied in its approach as anything since.

For example, we usually think of "Mannerism" as a late 16th century phenomenon. The Mannerists tended to exaggerate elements like scale and perspective and consequently their art is sometimes referred to as "affected". The Sicilian school of die engravers experimented with mannerism from about 470 to 450 BC. A silver tetradrachm from Leontini clearly illustrates the characteristics of this approach with a very mannered portrayal of Apollo. The pronounced jaw, lips and nose are complemented by a profile eye of incredibly distorted scale.

Leontini, AR tetradrachm (x2)
Mannerist style, ca. 450 BC.

The layered hair and oversized laurel wreath are also consistent with the mannered style. This experimentation, which occurs relatively early in the Classical period demonstrates that Greek numismatic art was anything but static.

Another stylistic convention, which 16th century artists termed "Baroque", is characterized by elaborate or ornate scrolls, curves and other symmetrical decoration. The Greeks, once again, had experimented with this approach in the late fifth century. On the Sicilian tetradrachm illustrated here, Apollo is fully facing so that the scroll-like ringlets of hair can fall evenly on each side. The hair is parted in the middle, and swept uniformly side to side. A laurel wreath rests on the back of Apollo's head,

Katana, AR tetradrachm (x2)
Baroque style, ca. 405 BC

emerging only at the sides in radiate fashion. Everything in this composition by the master engraver Choirion is in symmetrical balance. This celator was a contemporary of the famous Herakleidas, who also created a facing head of Apollo at Katana about five years before this piece was issued. Choirion's effort was the last design to come out of Katana, which fell under the siege of Dionysios I of Syracuse in 403.

The development of universally accepted proportions (canons) did much to give Greek art a distinctive look. In the early fourth century, artists followed the Canon of Polykleitos to scale the human anatomy. Polykleitos, from Argos, embodied his view of art as a science in a statue known as the *Doryphoros* (spear bearer). The concept of resting weight on one leg, referred to by art historians as contrapposto, was his invention. Dr. Carmen Arnold-Biucchi has clearly demonstrated the influence of Polykleitos and his works on coin die engravers (see bibliography). This canon, although much refined in comparison to archaic renderings of the human form, was still rather stiff and compact.

Lysippos, an artist from Sicyon, relaxed the canon by making extremities slimmer and more graceful, and the torso more lithe. Lysippos was the court sculptor to Alexander the Great, and apparently travelled with Alexander. One of his students, Chares of Lindos, created the statue known as the Colossus of Rhodes. By the middle of the fourth century, the Canon of Lysippos had become the accepted standard for representing the human form. At several cities, coins struck during this time show the transition from one canon to the other. This is not to say that we can precisely date the transition through coinage, but it is obvious that artists followed different canons as the series evolved. One of the most notable issues reflecting this change is the silver stater of the Lokroi Opontii with the Lokrian hero Ajax "the lesser" on the reverse. Aside

Lokris, AR tetradrachm
Canon of Polykleitos
(Classical Style)
ca. 369-338 BC

Lokris, AR tetradrachm
Canon of Lysippos
(Hellenistic Style)
ca. 369-338 BC

from the visual distinction of the two styles, there seems to be a corresponding change in epigraphy—perhaps denoting an interval between the early and later issues. On early issues bearing the Polykleitan styled Ajax, the reverse legend is invariably broken into two parts ΟΠΟΝ – ΤΙΩΝ or ΟΠΟΝΤΙ – ΩΝ. Later issues with the Lysippian styled Ajax render the ethnic in one unbroken word ΟΠΟΝΤΙΩΝ.

Because ancient Greek coins are wonderful works of art, as much as they are artifacts from antiquity, they are usually collected as such. It is possible to collect the series from an historical perspective, just as it is possible to collect Roman coins from an artistic perspective. It is usually the case, however, that lovers of art gravitate to the Greek series and lovers of history to the Roman. From an artistic point of view, there is little distinction between the collecting of coins and of engraved gems. The notable collectors of one invariably collected the other. This kinship of miniatures might be accounted for in terms of size, design, and aesthetic appeal; but their bond is much too strong to be explained in sensory terms alone. It is evident from the similarity of representations on certain ancient coins and gems that they must either have been designs from the same workshop or examples of coin die engravers and gem engravers independently borrowing a popular image. In Greece, some of the celators who engraved gems for the aristocracy probably engraved the dies for coins which circulated to the masses. This would seem to be confirmed by coins and gems of the 5th and 4th centuries bearing the signatures of Phrygillos, Olympios, and Euainetos. A study of images on ancient coins will therefore take one sooner or later to the field of engraved gems—if only for the joy of it.

BIBLIOGRAPHY
Artistry of the Celator

Alsop, Joseph. *The Rare Art Traditions*, Princeton University Press, 1982.
Arnold-Biucchi, Carmen. "Reflections of Polykleitos' Works on Ancient Coins", *Polykleitos, the Doryphoros, and Tradition*, Warren G. Moon, ed. University of Wisconsin Press, Madison, 1995.
Holloway, R. Ross. *A View of Greek Art*, Brown University Press, 1973.
Jex-Blake, K. Tr. *The Elder Pliny's Chapters on the History of Art*, Chicago, 1982.
Pausanias. *Guide to Greece*, 2 vols. Tr. Peter Levi, New York, 1985.
Pollitt, J.J. *The Ancient View of Greek Art*, Yale, 1974.
Richter, Gisela M.A. *The Sculpture and Sculptors of the Greeks*, Yale, 1930.
Seltman, Charles. *An Approach to Greek Art*, E.P. Dutton, New York, 1960.
Sutherland, C.H.V. *Art in Coinage*, London, 1955.

Celators who signed their works

From the time of the Italian Renaissance, when art collecting became a passion, works in any medium that have been signed by the artist have tended to be more popular than unsigned works. Greek artists of stature began signing their works at a very early date. Hundreds of signatures are recorded from Attic vases of the sixth and fifth centuries, and quite a surprising number of coin dies from various parts of the Greek world were signed by the celators who created and engraved their designs. Not surprisingly, coins struck from these dies have been and are still highly prized. Early numismatists recognized the signatures of Kimon, Euainetos and others on the magnificent silver coins of Sicily and Magna Graecia, but they were considered somewhat of an anomaly. Over the years, more and more signatures have been identified, and it is now clear that the practice, if not common, was at least more widespread than originally thought. Recent studies have suggested that even small bronze coins sometimes bear the artist's signature. This is a grand discovery for the collector with limited means, because these coins are often obtainable at quite reasonable price levels. Any collector who has admired the artistry of tiny Greek bronzes will not be surprised that they, like their touted and often pedigreed silver cousins, were executed by master die-engravers. In recent years, there has also been a growing recognition of artists signatures on dies from regions other than Sicily.

One might expect that, having identified signatures on certain bronze coins, numismatists will continue to discover additional examples or reinterpret some of the markings on others. Signatures are usually distinct from other names of an official nature in the manner that they are incorporated into the design. In at least two cases, the die-engraver (ΘΕΟΔΟΤΟΣ of Klazomenai, and ΝΕΥΑΝΤΟΣ of Kydonia in Crete) actually included the word ΕΠΟΕΙ (made [me]) after his name. This was a tradition among vase painters of the classical period and may be another indication of familiarity between the two disciplines. Despite this bold and apparently unique statement, celators names or abbreviated letters signifying the name of the celator were normally incorporated into the coin's design in a very subtle way. Of course this was in contrast to the names of kings or magistrates, which normally occupied a prominent place in the design.

Occasionally, celators of repute shared the chore and the signature of one will grace the obverse with that of the other on the reverse. A silver tetradrachm from Syracuse struck about 410 BC bears the signatures of Euainetos and Eumenos, while another struck at that city about five years later is signed by Euth[ymos] and Eumenos.

The following section lists some of the names, or abbreviated names, which seem to represent celator's signatures. These are in some cases conjectural, but many have been universally accepted as such. The list is not comprehensive by any means, but it helps to illustrate the widespread nature of this phenomenon.

ANAN...: an engraver at Messana in Sicily.

AP...: unknown by name, this celator who signed simply with the letters AP is perhaps the first artist known to sign a coin die. His work appears first in Leontini, and then in Syracuse (479 BC) where he is also referred to as the "Demareteion Master." His designs appear on the 50 litra Syracusan coin (dekadrachm) issued for Queen Demarete, as well as a tetradrachm of the same type and two other tetradrachms from Leontini.

AMI...: an engraver who worked at Metapontum in the last half of the fourth century (See also, the nomos with head of Leukippos in the section on Masterpieces).

ΑΠΟΛ...: engraved dies at Metapontum in Italy.

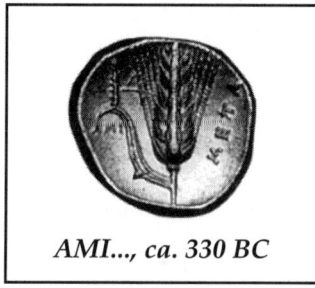
AMI..., ca. 330 BC

ΑΡΙ, ΑΡΙΣΤΟΞΕΝΟΣ: worked at Herakleia, Metapontum and perhaps Taras.

ATPI...: an engraver who worked at Massalia in Gaul.

ΔA...: Daidalos of Sicyon was a sculptor in marble and bronze and a relative of Polykleitos. He worked at Olympia and designed coins for the Olympic games of 420 BC.

Daidalos, ca. 400 BC

E, EY, EYA, ΕΥΑΙΝΕΤΟΣ: Euainetos, one of the ancient world's most highly regarded celators, worked at Syracuse and Katana in Sicily during the later years of the 5th century.

Euainetos, AR dekadrachm, ca. 390 BC

ΕΥΑΡΞΙΔΑΣ: Euarchidas, an engraver at Syracuse.

Ε, ΕΥΚ, ΕΥΚΛΕΙΔΑΣ: Eukleidas, a contemporary of Euainetos, in Sicily.

ΕΥΜ, ΕΥΜΕΝΟΥ: Eumenos engraved dies at Syracuse near the end of the fifth century.

ΕΥΘ...: Euthymos, an artist employed at Syracuse near the end of the fifth century.

Eumenos, ca. 410 BC

ΕΞ, ΕΞΑΚΕΣΤΙΔΑΣ: Exakestidas is famous for his designs on silver coins of Kamarina, and possibly designed and signed bronze coins for Syracuse as well.

ΗΡΑ...: on coins of Velia.

ΙΣΤΟΡΟΣ...: a signature on coins of Thourioi.

Exakestidas, ca. 410 BC

Kimon, AR dekadrachm, ca. 400 BC

K, KIMON: Kimon is considered by many to be the premier celator of classical Sicily. His masterful depiction of Arethusa, on a Syracusan silver dekadrachm of the late 5th century, set a standard which followers were hard pressed to emulate.

ΚΑΛ...: worked at Taras and Herakleia.

ΚΛΕ...: a signature at Thermai in Sicily.

ΚΛΕΥΔΩΡΟΥ: at Velia, Italy in the first half of the fourth century.

ΚΑΛ..., ca. 340 BC

ΚΡΑΤΕΣΙΠΠΟ: an engraver at Rhegion.

ΛΙΒΥΣ: possibly the earliest artist to sign a die from Thourioi.

ΛV...: a contemporary engraver of Exakestidas at Kamarina.

MA...: a possible signature appearing at Massalia in Gaul.

MAI..., ca. 410 BC

ΜΑΙ...: at Himera during the late fifth century.

ΜΙ, ΙΜ: a signature which appears at Syracuse, both on a silver tetradrachm and on bronze coins, is sometimes retrograde. Since the name of the artist is unknown, we can only speculate on the proper order of the letters.

ΜΟΛΟΣΣΟΣ: at Thourioi in Italy.

ΜΥΡ...: Myron was a master celator who worked at Akragas in Sicily about 410 BC. His galloping chariot obverse is paired with the famous reverse of two eagles perched over a dead hare.

Myron, ca. 410 BC

ΝΕΥΑΝΤΟΣ: a celator from Kydonia in Crete whose signature includes the word Epoei... (Made [me]).

ΝΙΚΑΡ...: worked at Taras about 280 BC.

NIKAP..., ca. 280 BC

ΝΙΚΑΝΔΡΟC: at Thourioi.

ΟΛΥΜ...: a signature from Arcadia.

Φ, ΦΡΥ, ΦΡΥΓΙΛΛΟΣ: Phrygillos was a prolific artist. He worked for several cities, including Thourioi, Terina, Hyele, Leontini, Velia and Syracuse during the last quarter of the fifth century.

The Π Master, ca. 400 BC.

ΦΙΛΙΣΤΙΩΝΟΣ: an engraver at the Italian cities of Herakleia, Velia and Terina.

ΦΙΛΟ...: at Herakleia, Lucania.

Π: the Π Master, worked at Terina ca. 400 BC.

ΠΑΡΜΕ...: Parmenides, at Syracuse.

Parmenides, ca. 405 BC

ΠΑΡ...: an engraver at Massalia in Gaul.

ΠΟΛΥ...: at Metapontum ca. 400-350 BC.

ΠΟΛΥ...: Polykrates?, engraved the reverse motif of two eagles perched over a dead hare—on a tetradrachm and probably on the dekadrachm of Akragas in Sicily.

Prokles, ca. 420 BC

ΠΡΟΚΛΕΣ: the signature of Prokles appears on coins at Katana and Naxos in Sicily.

ΠΥΘΟΔΩΡΟΥ: an engraver who worked at Aptera and Polyrhenion in Crete.

ΣΟΣΙΩΝ: Sosion is regarded as the first artist to sign a die at Syracuse.

Sosion, ca. 425 BC

ΘΕΟΔΟΤΟΣ: the signature of Theodotos, a celator from Klazomenai in Ionia, includes the word Epoei... (Made [me]).

ΧΑΡΙ...: a signature from Arcadia.

ΧΟΙΡΙΩΝ: Choirion engraved dies in a baroque style at Katana in Sicily.

Choirion, ca. 405 BC

BIBLIOGRAPHY
Celators who signed their works

Evans, A.J. *Syracusan medallions*, London, 1892.
Gallatin, A. *Syracusan Medallions of the Euainetos Type*, New York, 1930.
Head, Barclay V. *Historia Numorum*, London, 1911 (reprint, 1967).
Jongkees, J.H. *The Kimonian Decadrachms*, Utrecht, 1941.
Seltman, Charles T. *Masterpieces of Greek Coinage*, Oxford, 1949 (Obol reprint, 1980).
Seltman, Charles T. "The engravers of the Akragantine dekadrachms", *Numismatic Chronicle*, 1948.
Tudeer, L. "Die Tetradrachmenprägung von Syrakus in der Periode der signierenden Künstler", *Zeitschrift für Numismatik*, 1913.

Symbolism in Greek Art

The Greeks did not invent symbolism. A symbol is simply one thing that represents something else. Symbolism is usually a form of representing something which cannot be touched or seen. For as long as man has rendered images, even on rocks and cave walls, he has used this visual form of communication to convey esoteric ideas. The images found on Greek coins are absolutely full of symbolism and the study of these allusions can be very entertaining and instructive. The next few pages present a short list of subjects which are symbolic in nature, and a bibliography which will lead the reader to more complete sources.

Aegis: The goat skin shield of Zeus, used also by Athena and Apollo, was worn by Hellenistic kings as a symbol of the right to rule. It is usually seen knotted around the neck or draped over the shoulder.

Anchor: Symbol of stability. An attribute of the Seleukid kings of Syria.

Apple: The apple was a symbol of Aphrodite. It alludes to the judgement of Paris that she was the most beautiful of the Olympian goddesses. For that she won the prize of a golden apple.

Bee: A symbol of Demeter, the Queen Bee, whose priestesses were called Melissae (the bees). Also an emblem of Artemis, it was a symbol of virginity.

Boar: Sacred to Ares, and also an attribute of Demeter. The boar represented Winter, and the slaying of the Boar of Calydon was an allegorical allusion to the coming of Spring.

Bull horns: In classical times, bull horns were considered a reference to Dionysos. The deity is known by many epithets which relate to the bull. One of these was "two-horned", an epithet also used to honor Alexander the Great. Demetrios Poliorketes and Seleukos I were depicted wearing bull's horns on tetradrachms issued during their reigns. Whether this symbolism alluded to Dionysos or to Alexander is unclear. Bull horns also were used to indicate river gods, especially in fifth century coinage of Sicily.

Cock: A symbol of vigilance and pugnacity. Sacred to Apollo, Asklepios, Ares, Hermes, Priapos and Athena.

Dove: Symbolized the renewal of life. Zeus was fed by doves. A dove with an olive branch is a symbol of Athena. The bird is sacred to Dionysos, and it is a symbol of Aphrodite.

Eagle: An attribute of Zeus, and all sky gods. It symbolizes royalty and victory—especially with a snake in its talons.

Elephant Scalp: This convention does not appear prior to its adoption on posthumous coins of Alexander, therefore it seems likely that it is an allusion to the Eastern victories of the great conqueror. By extension, it seems to have become a symbol of military strength to some of his successors—particularly in the Ptolemaic and Seleukid dynasties.

Goat: A symbol of virility. It is sacred to Artemis and Zeus, and an attribute of Dionysos. Zeus was suckled by the goat Amalthea.

Grain: Corn and wheat, and occasionally other grains, symbolized fertility and abundance. The sheaf or wreath of grain was an attribute of Demeter.

Grapes: The symbol of Dionysos, god of wine. Sometimes depicted as a wreath of leaves or as a bunch of hanging fruit.

Gryphon: Sacred to Apollo as a solar reference, to Athena as a symbol of wisdom and to Nemesis as a representation of vengeance.

Hare: The hare is associated with the lunar goddess Hekate. Also considered a messenger and as such is an attribute of Hermes.

Ivy: Sacred to Dionysos, who is often crowned with ivy. It represents eternal life, revelry and constant affection.

Laurel: The tree sacred to Apollo, signifies peace, truce or victory. The small leaved bay laurel was used for making victory crowns.

Lion Scalp: This symbol was so popularized in the coinage of Alexander the Great that it is difficult to think of it as an attribute of Herakles. Nevertheless, coins struck more than a century before Alexander's birth bear the image of Herakles wearing a lion's scalp. The connection between Alexander and Herakles, both of whom were mortals that earned immortality through deification, is obvious.

Oak: The tree sacred to Zeus.

Pan: A personification of lust and the outdoors. Associated figures include satyrs, maenads and centaurs.

Phrygian Cap: A short conical headpiece relating to the cult worship of Mithras in the East. Worn originally by the priests of Mithras—the magi—but used later to portray kings and minor deities. It is a general symbol of the East.

Pomegranate: A symbol of fertility (because of its many seeds) and immortality. It was the emblem of Hera, and of Demeter and Persephone as Spring renewal. It is the plant which supposedly grew from the blood of Dionysos.

Ram Horns: An attribute of Zeus Ammon, the ram's horns were added to the posthumous portrait of Alexander on coins of his generals Ptolemy I and Lysimachos. This visual reference to Alexander's touted relationship with Zeus is nearly unique in Greek numismatics. Another rare example appears in the coinage struck in honor of Arsinoe II, the sister and wife of Ptolemy II, who claimed to be the daughter of Zeus Ammon. Her portrait is sometimes rendered with the horn of Ammon in her hair.

Scepter: A symbol of authority from very early times.

Sun and Moon: To the early Greeks the sun represented Helios, and the moon his sister Selene. In later times, Apollo came to be associated with the sun, and his sister Artemis (Roman Diana) with the moon. They shared the heavens, with Helios/Apollo driving a quadriga across the sky from morning to evening and Selene/Artemis taking over in the evening. The Sun is a personification of truth.

Thunderbolt: An attribute and weapon of Zeus, who hurled the thunderbolt (lightning) like a spear.

Torch: A symbol of life, and an attribute of Ceres who searches for her daughter Persephone.

BIBLIOGRAPHY
Symbolism in Greek Art

Baldwin, Agnes. *Symbolism on Greek Coins,* (Durst reprint) New York, 1977.
Black, Jeremy and Anthony Green. *Gods, Demons and Symbols of Ancient Mesopotamia, An Illustrated Dictionary,* Austin, 1992.
Cirlot, J.E. *A Dictionary of Symbols,* (english translation) London, 1962.
Cooper, J.C. *An Illustrated Encycoplaedia of Traditional Symbols,* London, 1978.
Hall, James. *Dictionary of Subjects & Symbols in Art,* New York, 1974.
Piper, Sir David. *The Random House Dictionary of Art and Artists,* New York, 1988.
Wittkower, Rudolf. *Allegory and the Migration of Symbols,* London, 1977.

Canting Puns

It was not uncommon for Greek cities to adopt coin motifs with punning references to their name. To the modern world these are canting puns. That is, they are unrecognizable as such due to our lack of familiarity with the language. To the ancient Greeks, they would not have been obscure at all. This sort of novelty is similar in a way to the creation of optical illusions or the creation of fanciful creatures. Listed below are a few of the cities that issued coins with punning references.

Akragas: Crab

Aspendos: Slinger

Delphi: Dolphin

Himera: Rooster

Klazomenai: Sound of a Swan

Laos: Thrush

Leontini: Lion

Melos: Apple

Phokaia: Seal

Rhodos: Rose

Selinus: Parsley—rock celery

Side: Pomegranate

Tauromenion: Bull

Trapezos: Table

Zankle: Sickle—for its harbor shape

* For additional information see: Elbers, G.C.A. "Canting Puns on Ancient Greek Coins", *SAN*, Vol. XV, No. 1, 1984.

Aspendos, AR stater ca. 370-330 BC "Slinger"

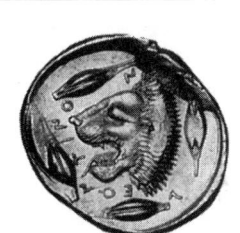

Leontini, AR tetradrachm ca. 455-430 BC

Zankle, AR drachm ca. 520-500 BC "Sickle Harbor"

Optical Trickery

Not all Greek numismatic art was religious or political, or for that matter serious. A number of coin types reveal a playful experimentation with images and a surprisingly good understanding of perspective. As if the unusual designs were not themselves difficult enough, they often were engraved for tiny fractional coinage.

On a billon stater from the island of Lesbos, the foreparts of two confronted lions are arranged so that they form a third feline head which faces the viewer. This coin was struck during the sixth century and demonstrates a sophisticated level of experimentation very early in the development of coinage.

A rare hemidrachm from an uncertain mint, also on the island of Lesbos, depicts two wild boar confronted so that their heads become one. Viewed singly, they each present a boar's head in profile. Viewed as a composite, they form a single facing head.

A silver nomos from Cumae, in Campania, combines three animals to produce one facing image. In the center, a Lion's head is shown from a somewhat elevated perspective. Alongside the lion are the foreparts of two boars, each of which wraps to the contour of the feline head.

The tiny obol (.68 grams) from an uncertain Cilician mint illustrates a form of optical trickery that probably originated in three dimensional sculpture—perhaps a Herm. The tricephalic (three headed) image reflects only a two dimensional plane, but the sculptural object would have had a fourth side, which faced to the back. Therefore, the illusion of a facing head was created from all four viewing quarters.

Lesbos, Billon stater ca. 550-500 BC

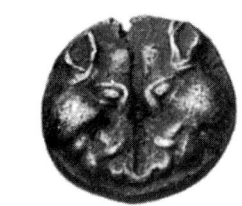
Lesbos, AR hemidrachm ca. 500-480 BC (x2)

Cumae, AR nomos ca. 420-380 BC

Cilicia, Uncertain mint AR obol (x4), ca. 4th c. BC

Senescence in Numismatic Art

Throughout history there have been a number of rulers who came to power in their youth and left it in their twilight years. As portraits were prepared for coinage that was issued at regular intervals, the aging of these dignitaries was revealed on their coins. To the historian, this scrapbook of portraits may be considered a fortunate accident. But in some cases, the treatment of age and aging has been purposeful and an artistic convention in itself. Analyzing the depictions of gods and goddesses, who are supposedly immortal and ageless, can provide some interesting results.

One series that reveals the aging of a goddess is the group of Macedonian tetradrachms with obverse depictions of Artemis centered on a Macedonian shield. Ranging from youth to maturity, Artemis is presented here as ageless in the sense that she is *every* age. These coins were all struck at the same time, and the same place, as hoard evidence verifies. With a little effort, one could easily extend the range of ages represented beyond the four shown here. It is possible, of course, for different engravers to render the subject in different ways, but it is unlikely that such a wide range of conceptions could have existed within the same workshop. It is more likely that this representation of aging was intentional, although probably not in a narrative sense.

Was marked difference in portrayal an attempt by celators in Macedon to hone portrait skills at a time when there were not any regal portraits on their coins? Was it just playfulness? Was it accidental and only the product of varying celatorial perceptions? Whatever the cause, or celator's motivation, this phenomenon and others like it provide fertile ground for the collector, student and scholar to explore.

Artemis as a child

Artemis as a young lady

Artemis full-grown

Artemis at maturity

Greek Dress and Hair Styles

The gods and goddesses, not to mention kings and queens, of ancient Greece were very often depicted wearing distinctive clothing, or with their hair coiffured in a popular way. Headdresses of a great variety were also used to designate divinity, a state of mourning or some other state of being. Some of these methods of portrayal, *costumes* if you will, were popularized by the Greek theater. Plays were a major form of recreation in the Greek world, especially during the Classical Period and later. It was necessary in a play that the characters be recognized by sight, therefore certain forms of dress and hairstyle became associated with individual deities or classes of divinities, and mortals as well. This is an incredibly interesting subject for the numismatist, and it is unfortunate that we can only discuss a few examples here. Although some of the references listed in the bibliography are quite old and out of print, they are very useful and we encourage the reader to use interlibrary loan facilities to obtain copies for research.

 The *ampyx* is a band worn on the forehead and tied behind to confine the hair. It was often made of precious metal and adorned with gems. In Lydia, men were said to have worn the ampyx, but on coins it is usually, if not always, seen on women. The nymph on a tetradrachm from Segesta wears both an ampyx and sphendone.

Segesta, Sicily, ca. 400 BC, Nymph with hair in Ampyx and Sphendone

 *Korymbos* means literally, a bunch of ivy berries, and was at first used to describe a form of garland. It later became a popular hair style, in which the hair is pulled back and tied at the top of the head. It is typically seen on depictions of Aphrodite, like this one from Syracuse, and also of Artemis.

Syracuse, ca. 445 BC, Arethusa with hair tied in a Korymbos

 The *saccos* was a woman's hair net. Nets in general were called Kekryphaloi, and sometimes (as on a famous tetradrachm by Kimon) they were made of loosely woven ribbon. The sakkos was a solid piece of cloth which was tied at the end by a ribbon. There were many different ways to tie the sakkos, which gave it a different appearance at times. The sakkos in the line drawing above is worn with a *stephane* (metal band).

Corinth, ca. 330-300 BC
Aphrodite with hair in Saccos

 The *sphendone*, like the stephane (two different words in Greek), was a hair fastener, or sort of diadem, which sat above the forehead almost like a crown. The sphendone is, in fact, the equivalent of the Latin corona. Its Greek name comes from the similarity in appearance to a sling.

Kyzikos, ca. 350 BC
Aphrodite with hair in Sphendone

BIBLIOGRAPHY
Greek Dress and Hair Styles

Bieber, Margarete. *The History of The Greek and Roman Theater,* Princeton, 1961.
Evans, Maria Millington. *Chapters on Greek Dress,* Macmillan, London/New York, 1893.
Guhl, E. and W. Koner. *The Greeks and Romans, Their Life and Customs,* (reprint) London, 1989.
Miller, Walter. *Daedalus and Thespis, The Contributions of the Ancient Dramatic Poets to Our Knowledge of the Arts and Crafts of Greece,* New York, 1929.
Peck, Harry Thurston. Ed. *Harper's Dictionary of Classical Literature and Antiquities,* New York, 1896.

Mythology and Coin Motifs

Across the spectrum of numismatic art there are many themes of interest to collectors, but one of the most popular is the illustration of mythological tales. Nearly all mythological stories started in an oral tradition, even before the advent of the written word. They were sometimes acted out, and the plays themselves became graphic illustrations of the narrative. These ageless stories gradually acquired more or less standard illustrations that could be understood by all who saw them. They were in a sense *master images*, which reflected the essence of Greek culture, politics, and religion. Greek artists were constantly attempting to define the essence of specific forms and symbols. These were a people obsessed with discovery of the cosmological order of all things. Their idealism lies at the heart of Greek art, at least through the Classical Period.

Why do certain images speak to us with such power? Conventions of representation, over a long period of time, become part of our visual vocabulary. Just as the philosopher translates the sensory world into aesthetic principles, the artist translates aesthetic concepts into sensory images. Some of these master images appeared first in the Archaic Period and continued to be employed throughout Greek history. Many were adopted by the Romans and nonclassical cultures with little or no modification. Although commonly seen in other forms of art, which usually catered to wealthy patrons, these images very often found their way to the whole of society, the external world, and posterity through their presence on coinage. It has often been said the ancient coins were the "newspapers" of their day—perhaps the Time Magazine of their day would be a better analogy.

The production of coins in ancient Greece was considered by the ancients themselves as a major form of artistic expression. Consequently, the artists engraving dies for coins were as much in tune with the standard forms of expression as any other artist would be. In many cases, those forms envisaged some mystic concept. Myth, after all, is the embodiment of the ethnic conscience and a picture is worth a thousand words. The collecting of coins with mythological narrative is a fascination shared by many, and it is a field that surprisingly is still open to research. There are thousands of individual and group scenes on ancient coins that have not to this day been adequately explained. The student or scholar who looks at a single episode, and then examines the wide spectrum of motifs, will typically find something new and exciting. This sense of discovery is intensely gratifying to most collectors, because it satisfies the same innate drives that make armchair travel and Walter Mitty exploration a popular pastime.

Herakles and the Nemean Lion

One of the most popular of all mythological heroes is Herakles (Hercules in Latin). The stories of this hero are filled with power and emotion, and have always served as a representation of virtue. Herakles, in the tale by Xenophon, chose to follow Virtue rather than Pleasure and accepted a life of great toil in exchange for immortality.

According to legend, Herakles in a fit of madness killed his own children by Megara, and two children of his half-brother Iphicles. In remorse, Herakles sentenced himself to exile and was subsequently purified by Thespius. The Oracle at Delphi ordered that he should serve Eurystheus, king of the Mycenaeans, for a period of twelve years. During this time he was obligated to perform twelve great labors, the first of which was the killing of the monstrous lion that terrorized the valley of Nemea.

Finding his weapons powerless because of the lion's invulnerable skin, Herakles finally strangled it with his bare hands. He skinned the lion with its own claws, because no knife would cut it, and in future adventures wore the scalp as a helmet and skin as armor. The depiction of Herakles wearing the lion's scalp was a popular and enduring motif.

A study of narrative scenes in which Herakles strangles the Nemean Lion must begin with a consideration of the media in which these depictions are found. The scene occurs most often in one of three basic designs; horizontal, vertical, or circular. Each was particularly well suited to a specific application. Some of the earliest illustrations of the myth are to be found in Attic black-figure vase painting. Indeed, within this medium all three of the above motifs may be seen. The oldest examples, on narrow vases, portray

Archaic

Herakles in Lion's Scalp
Dikaia, ca. 490 BC

Classical

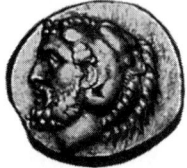

Herakles in Lion's Scalp
Kos, ca. 366-300 BC

Hellenistic

Herakles in Lion's Scalp
Syracuse, 214-212 BC

Herakles and the lion standing upright in a distinctly vertical plane. The figures stretched out parallel to the ground best fit the design of wide bodied vases or the horizontal neck panels of kraters and amphorae. This technique of representation was first introduced in the mid to late 6th century by the incomparable Exekias. The last to come on the scene was the circular motif, which was relatively rare and to my knowledge used only in kylix tondo designs. The horizontal motif seems not to have enjoyed any long term popularity, possibly because of the inferior position of Herakles. It lacks the sense of power and heroic conquest felt in the vertical and circular motifs. Another probable cause of its fading popularity was the shortage of applications in which an artist could utilize that format. By the mid 5th century it seems to have lost any major influence that it might previously have had.

On the other hand, the vertical motif was extremely popular on fifth century carved gems, which unquestionably played an important role in the development of the numismatic image. It was this variation that the celator Phrygillos brought to the silver didrachms of Lucania about 400 BC. J.P. Six proposed in the late 19th century that this style should be traced to a bronze sculpture by Myron.

Although the vertical image was very powerful, and well accepted, the circular space on coins presented the same compositional problems as the earlier kylix tondo. The result was a new wave of experimentation with the circular motif. This movement is very well illustrated in a gold stater of Syracuse designed by the celator Euainetos. These staters reflect the ultimate in artistic utilization of a circular space. The image literally radiates energy in all directions, contained only by the invisible barrier of the surface itself.

Syracuse, AV stater ca. 400 BC, by Euainetos

As powerful and well suited as this innovative design was, it did not totally supplant the vertical arrangement. Contemporary staters of Mallos and Tarsos, two neighboring cities in Cilicia, illustrate the acceptance of both renditions. Note that the image from Tarsus is reversed—perhaps because it was copied directly from the Syracusan coin.

Despite their differing orientations, these narrative scenes often share some common artistic features. The lion's raised foot, pushing against the

Mallos, AR stater ca. 380 BC

Tarsos, AR stater ca. 370 BC

knee of Herakles is a recurrent ploy that dates back to the 6th century BC. It was used consistently in both vertical and circular motifs, on coins and vases. There can be little doubt that artists understood its psychological significance. The futility of the lion's struggle seems to be embodied in this simple act. Another major aspect of this composition is the positioning of Herakles over the lion, so that his locked arms not only encircle the lion's throat, but lift the weight of its body as well. Even in the circular motifs, where that lifting of weight is less obvious, the artist often added a ground line to emphasize the superior position of Herakles.

The myth of Herakles and the Nemean lion was reflected during ancient times in virtually every field of artistic endeavor. Vase painters, gem carvers, metal workers, and die sinkers all shared in experimentation with new motifs on a variety of surfaces and planes. Through continued presence and widespread acceptance of the motif, it became a Master Image that reflected the power of the soul, transcending all of the weapons and power of man or nature.

The 12 Labors of Herakles were:
- Killing the Nemean Lion
- Killing the Hydra
- Catching the Erymanthian Boar
- Capturing the Hind of Ceryneia
- Driving away the Stymphalian Birds
- Cleaning the Stables of Augias
- Capturing the Bull of Crete
- Stealing the Horses of Diomedes
- Fetching the Belt of Hippolyte
- Killing Geryon
- Collecting the Golden Apples of the Hesperides
- Capturing Cerberus

Herakles and the Hydra
Labor #2
Phaistos, Crete
AR stater, ca. 350 BC

Herakles went on to complete all twelve of the assigned labors, and eventually gained immortality. The task took its toll however. On a tetradrachm issued by Antiochos I of Syria the "Weary Herakles" sits slumped forward on a rock, resting against his club in a pensive pose. This theme was also the subject of a famous marble statue by the Athenian sculptor Glykon.

Antiochos I, Syria
AR tetradrachm
280-261 BC

The Rape of Kassandra

One of the little heralded, but extremely important, figures in Homer's *Iliad* was Ajax, the son of King Oileus of Lokris. Ajax fought with the Greeks in the Trojan War and became a local hero. He should not be confused with the mighty Ajax of Salamis, who was the friend of Achilles—and the Lokrian is often referred to as "the lesser" for this reason. As the city of Troy was under assault, Ajax raped the prophetess Kassandra (daughter of King Priam) on the altar of Athena. In doing so, he not only defiled a temple priestess but knocked over the revered Palladium and desecrated the temple itself—not a smart thing to do!

In retribution, the enraged Athena conspired with her brother Poseidon to wreck the Greek fleet as it departed for home. Upon setting sail, many ships were blown off course in a violent storm conjured up by the gods. The ship bearing Ajax foundered and was lost, but he managed to swim to a nearby rock. Standing on the rock, he haughtily proclaimed that not even the gods could kill him! Poseidon directed a bolt of lightning at the rock, which split in two, and Ajax was drowned.

The story ends there for the insolent Ajax, but this same storm blew the ship of Odysseos so far off course that he spent another ten years wandering in search of home. Ironically, the imprudent action of Ajax provided the great sequel to Homer's tale.

The story of Ajax's misadventure is referred to in Greek art as the Rape of Kassandra. It is a recurrent theme and seems to have held no specific geographical attachment. Narrative scenes of Ajax and Kassandra appear on painted vases of all types, and from a fairly early period. The scene also appears on carved gemstones—including one that is believed to copy a painting by Apollodotos. It is arguably represented on a gold Skythian gorytus (bow case), with scenes of the Trojan War, found in the tomb of Philip II at Vergina. In virtually all depictions of this myth, Ajax is portrayed as a helmeted lunging warrior, bearing a short sword in his right hand.

This standard representation of the hoplite appears on a silver stater of Lokris, struck at Opus during the latter half of the fourth century, and also on a bronze coin struck at Skarphea in Lokris about the same time. One stater die includes the name AIAS (Ajax) below the figure. The type does not originate there, however, as we can see on earlier works of art. The same convention, in a more archaic style, appeared on a stater of Aspendos about 100 years earlier. The nature of the image is rather generic, and can only be identified as Ajax with confidence when presented in a broader context.

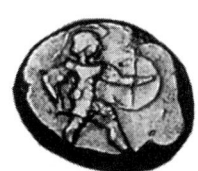

*Aspendos, AR stater
ca. 460-420 BC*

*Ajax, the lesser, son of Oileus
on a silver tetradrachm of the Opontii in Lokris*

Oedipus and the Sphinx

The Oracle at Delphi warned Laios, King of Thebes, that in retribution for having kidnapped a son of Pelops, he would be killed by his own son. Alarmed by this, Laios exposed his newborn son Oedipus (Oidipeus in Greek) on Mount Kithairon. The baby was rescued by shepherds and taken to Corinth, where he was adopted by King Polybos. Having grown up as a son of the Corinthian king, Oedipus learned that his fate was to bring destruction upon his family by killing his father and marrying his own mother. To avoid this, he left Corinth and what he thought to be his family. On his journey through the mountains of Boeotia he encountered an old man [King Laios] who tried to divert his path. They struggled and the old man fell mortally wounded.

Just outside the gates of Thebes, Oedipus met the legendary Sphinx—a seated monster from Ethiopia, with the face of a young girl, body of a lion, wings and talons of an eagle and a serpent's tail. The Sphinx posed a question to all passersby and tore them to pieces if they could not answer. Only the correct answer to the Sphinx's riddle would

rid the city of this dreaded scourge. The new king, Kreon, promised the hand of Iokaste (his sister and widow of Laios) to anyone who answered the riddle correctly. The riddle of the Sphinx was "What walks on four legs in the morning, two at noon and three in the evening?" Oedipus answered "Man—first as an infant on all fours, then as man on two legs and lastly as an old man leaning on a staff." The vanquished Sphinx destroyed itself and Oedipus was married to Iokaste (his mother) fulfilling the prophecy. The story goes on, but we will leave it here. This mythical tale is very old, having been related in the Odyssey and by Hesiod. It was the subject of later works by Sophocles, Aeschylus, and Seneca.

The Sphinx was a recurring theme on the coinage of Chios, a large Aegean island opposite Klazomenai. The city of Chios was a cultural center as well as a prosperous commercial port. It laid claim to being the birthplace of Homer, but this is uncertain. It was, however, the home of the Greek historian Theopompus—a protégé of Alexander the Great, and (by some accounts) of the bucolic poet Theocritus. The reason for the appearance of the Sphinx on Chian coinage is uncertain, but the motif lasted there nearly five hundred years. Barclay Head (*Historia Numorum*) postulated that it probably symbolized the cult worship of Dionysos. We lack any other reasonable explanation as to why it became heraldic.

The Sphinx also appears on the coinage of other Greek cities, including those illustrated here.

Lycia, AR stater
ca. 480-440 BC

Chios, AR tetradrachm
ca. 420-350 BC

Chios, AR drachm
ca. 190-84 BC

Kaunos, AE 13mm
ca. 350-309 BC

Perge, AE 13mm
ca. 2nd century BC

Theseus and the Minotaur

Theseus and the Minotaur from an Attic vase

Theseus was the great national hero of Attica. He was raised, according to legend, in Troizen (In the Peloponnesos across the Saronic Gulf from Aigina) and came to Athens as a young man in search of fame. He tried to emulate Herakles by disposing of an assortment of robbers and monsters that infested the countryside. He was a part of nearly all the great heroic expeditions. He was an Argonaut, captured the bull of Marathon, took part in the Calydonian Boar hunt, fought with the Lapiths against the Centaurs and helped steal Helen from Sparta. The list of his exploits goes on and on. One of the most famous of his heroic deeds, was the slaying of the Minotaur, a monster with a human body and a bull's head. The Minotaur was kept in a specially designed Labyrinth at the palace of Minos in Crete. Minos waged war on the Athenians, and as tribute they were required to send him seven youths and seven maidens each year—to be devoured in the Labyrinth. Theseus slew the Minotaur and freed Athens from this horror.

The Minotaur and the labyrinth were frequent subjects on the coinage of Knossos in Crete. Hera also was worshipped there and she appears along with the labyrinth on silver coins of the fourth century.

Knossos, Crete, AR stater ca. 440 BC

Knossos, Crete, AR stater ca. 320 BC

Europa and the Bull

Europa was a daughter of king Agenor of Phoenicia. According to tradition, she and her maidens were relaxing one day at a spot on the seashore when Zeus saw them and fell in love with her (not an uncommon thing for Zeus to do). Being able to change into any form he desired, he appeared before them in the form of a bull and reclined at Europa's feet. She playfully mounted the bull's back, whereupon he rushed into the sea and with her seated on his back swam to the island of Crete. There, she was ravished by him in a spring grove. In honor of the occasion, the trees of this grove were forever allowed to keep their leaves. By Zeus, she became the mother of Minos, Rhadamanthus and Sarpedon. Europa later married Asterion, the king of Crete, and when she died was deified by the gods and became a constellation in the heavens.

Narrative art appears very early in the evolution of coinage, and stories like this one made excellent subjects for the celator. A tiny silver fraction from Macedon, struck about 480 BC, depicts a narrative combination of two images. The female head in profile, with its archaic ringlets of hair and oval eye, is accompanied by the forepart of a bull. This pairing probably alludes to the mythological tale of Europa and the bull. In other words, the

Europa and the bull?
Macedon, ca. 480 BC

images are a catalyst for the recalling of an important oral and literary tradition. A later issue, from Phaistos in Crete, shows the extent to which narrative had developed during the Classical Period. In this composition Europa actually seems to be in conversation with the bull (Zeus).

Europa and the bull Phaistos, ca. 350 BC

The island of Crete is known as a prolific center of narrative art and the composition on this silver stater exemplifies that tradition. Again, the mythological story of Europa served as the inspiration for this design, which actually appears at Gortyna a bit earlier than the specimen illustrated. This coin's obverse portrays Europa in a grove of trees whose leaves are clearly displayed. The trunk of the tree she rests in takes on the form of an eagle's head (another common guise of Zeus). On the reverse is the metamorphosed Zeus as a bull. The story of Europa appears also on coins of Phoenicia, her original home.

Gortyna, Crete, AR stater, ca. 350-300 BC

BIBLIOGRAPHY
Mythology and Coin Motifs

Cammann, Jean B. Numismatic Mythology, New York, 1936.
Frame, Douglas. *The Myth of Return in Early Greek Epic.*, Yale, 1978.
Gardner, Percy. *The Types of Greek Coins*, London, 1883 (1965 reprint).
Grant, Michael. *Myths of the Greeks and Romans*, New York, 1964.
Grimal, Pierre. *The Dictionary of Classical Mythology*, tr. A.R. Maxwell-Hyslop, Oxford, 1988.
Hamilton, Edith. *Mythology*, New York, 1953.
Morford, M.P.O. and R. J. Lenardon. *Classical Mythology*, NY, 1977.
Sayles, W.G. "The Locrian Ajax: Stylistic Change in the Fourth Century B.C.", *SAN*, Vol. XVI, No. 2, 1985.

Athletes and Athletic Events

Athletic contests were important in Greek society, since they were derived mainly from the training of a Hoplite for war. The term *agonistikos* means combatant or contestant interchangeably. Successful athletes at the agonistic games were akin to heroes and gods. In Greek art, early renderings of the male form emphasize (one might say over emphasize) muscular development. While this may in part be artistic naiveté, it is probably also the reflection of a preoccupation with athleticism or *arete*. This term embodies the spirit of competition—which require prowess, skill, valor and a host of other virtues bestowed on the faithful by *Agon,* the god of the games.

There were scores of games held throughout Greece, but the most important of them were the annual Pan-Hellenic games, open to all (and only) qualified Greek citizens. They were held on a rotational basis at Olympia, Nemea, Corinth and Delphi, and were respectively called the Olympic, Nemean, Isthmian and Pythian games.

The theme of athletic competition as a coin motif is one that many collectors find appealing. Included here are a few additional types which are games related.

Philip II, ca. 356 BC
AR tetradrachm

Philip II, ca. 348 BC
AV stater

Horse racing was an Olympic event of great prestige and intense competition. It was a great honor for Philip II of Macedon to gain entry to the games, since they were open only to Greeks. Prior to that time, the Macedonians were considered by other Greeks as barbarians. It was an even greater honor for Philip's horses to win the prize. In 356 BC his entry won the single horse event, and in 348 the two horse chariot event. Both of these victories were proudly announced (should we say propagandized) by placing references to them on the reverses of his coins struck in gold, silver and bronze. Plutarch tells us that this was indeed his intention: "[Philip] ...had victories of his chariots at Olympia stamped on his coins." The rider on this tetradrachm takes a victory lap with palm branch in hand.

Among the many events held at the Pan-Hellenic games, wrestling was one of the most popular. The Greek form of the sport involved the taking down of an opponent from the standing position in a three-fall contest. This event was the theme of a wonderful series of silver staters struck at Aspendos in Asia Minor during the mid 4th century. A series of dies depicts the contest at various stages. Presented here are four specimens tracking the progress of a match in stop-action animation.

The first specimen (top) shows two wrestlers as they are about to engage. The second shows them grappling, with the figure on the left gaining a superior hold. On the third specimen, the contestant on the right reaches into the abdomen of his opponent and gains a reversal of advantage. In scene four, the left figure has reestablished control as the one on the right attempts a trip for the take down. There are probably additional panels to this fascinating kaleidoscope.

The series from Aspendos is not the earliest representation of agonistic wrestlers on a coin. A unique Thraco-Macedonian silver fraction of the late sixth century bears two wrestlers about to engage—an indistinct object between them. In an article published in *The International Journal of the History of Sport*, December 1993), Anthony Milavic suggests that this object is a prize cauldron. The cauldron was depicted on 6th century Attic black-figure vases as a wrestler's prize, and a contemporary date for this coin seems stylistically consistent. It is the cauldron that marks this piece as an agonistic rather than mythological scene.

Agonistic wrestlers are actually scarce in Greek numismatics. Aside from these issues from Aspendos and Macedon, only two other cities, Selge and Etenna, depict wrestling scenes which are games related.

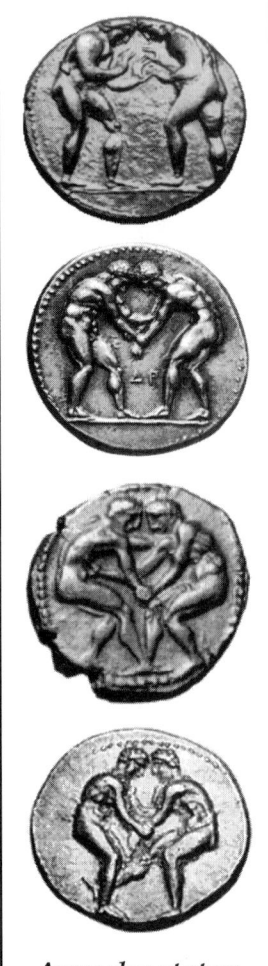

Aspendos staters

Thraco-Macedonian, uncertain mint AR trihemiobol (x2), late 6th century

The diskobolos (discus thrower) was a participant at the games of ancient Greece from very early times. The event was originally a part of the Pentathlon, added to the Olympic program in 708 BC, and later became a single event. The athlete depicted here is starting his spin to gather momentum before releasing the discus. The discus was made originally of stone, and later was cast from iron and bronze. All contestants used the same discus in competition. One Olympic pentathlete, Phayllos, reportedly threw the discus 95 feet. Another is said to have thrown a discus across the Alpheos—a major river in that part of the Peloponnesos. These contests were a part of the festivals and games held in many parts of the Greek world, not just at the Pan-Hellenic games. The tripod cauldron shown on this coin was awarded as a prize to the winner at the Triopian games. These contests were held in honor of Apollo Triopios by the five cities of the Dorian Pentapolis—Kos, Knidos, Ialysos, Lindos and Kamiros.

Kos, AR tetradrachm ca. 450 BC

Kelenderis, AR stater ca. 370 BC

Kyzikos, EL stater, ca. 340 BC

A contest which translates roughly as the "ride and run" was another athletic event which owed its origin to military training. In this event, the rider circled the hippodrome several times and then for the final lap was required to dismount the horse and lead it on foot. The contestant originally was required to carry two spears and a shield, but this obviously militaristic feature was later discarded. The event, though it was dropped from the Olympic program in 444 BC, is depicted on a number of Greek coins, two of which are shown here. One type from Taras shows the rider dismounting with spears and shield. On the specimen from Kelenderis, the horse rears as it is stopped abruptly for the dismount.

Kyzikos
EL 1/6 stater
ca. 450-400 BC

The hoplite race in armor was one of the athletic events clearly derived from the training of a young man for war. Scenes of the "hoplitodromos" appear on Attic vases, and this electrum fraction depicts a contestant at the starting line. For a complete history of the race, and a compelling argument for attribution of this motif, see Anthony Milavic's article in *The Celator*, Vol. 5, No. 8 (August 1991).

In contrast to the flashy chariots of the two-horse and four-horse races, one early event in the Olympic program was a two-mule cart race. This event was won in the 480 Olympics by Anaxilaos, the tyrant of Rhegion and Messana. He commemorated the victory on his coins, and although the event was dropped in 444, it was still being touted on the coinage of Messana at the end of the century, as evidenced on this specimen.

Messana
AR tetradrachm
ca. 400 BC

BIBLIOGRAPHY
Athletes and Athletic Events

Crowther, Nigel B. "Studies in Greek Athletics", *Classical World* 78 (1984) and 79 (1985).

Finley, M.I., and Pleket, H.W., *The Olympic Games: The First Thousand Years*, New York, 1966.

Gardiner, E.N. *Athletics of the Ancient World*, Oxford, 1930.

Harris, H.A. *Greek Athletes and Athletics*, University of Indiana, 1966.

Kyle, Donald. *Athletics in Ancient Athens*, Leiden, 1987.

Milavic, Anthony F. "Ancient Olympia: The Place, The Games", *The Celator*, July 1992 and "The First Greek Wrestler-type Coin", *The Celator*, February 1993.

Miller, Stephen G. *ARETE, Greek Sports From Ancient Sources*, Berkeley, 1991.

Poliakoff, M.B. *Combat Sports in the Ancient World*, New Haven, 1987.

Robinson, R.S. *Sources for the History of Greek Athletics in English Translation*, Chicago, 1979 (reprint).

Scanlon, Thomas F. *Greek and Roman Athletics, A Bibliography*, Chicago, 1984.

The Periods of Greek Art

It never occurred to the Greeks that there was an Archaic Period or a Classical Period, nor did they think of themselves as a nation—much less citizens of the Hellenistic Period. They understood the concept of antiquity, and of historical or even art historical relationships, but the "Periods of Greek Art" are a creation of the modern age. The subject of *archaizing* was mentioned briefly in the preceding chapter about dating, and really deserves a treatise in its own right. It will have to suffice for us to say that this phenomenon proves that artists of the ancient world were, like the artists of today, respectful of the work which preceded their own. On ancient coins, there are numerous examples of what can only be seen as intentional reverence for prior generations—both in the selection of motifs, and the manner of representation. In some cases they repeated, as faithfully as possible, the techniques of the age that they themselves considered golden. In other cases, as exemplified in the Winged Carian on page 164, the artist modernized an earlier motif in a way that paid tribute. Greek artists were certainly aware of the changes taking place in their world of images, but these changes could not be put into perspective until much later.

Because Greek coins are justifiably considered works of art, the field of Greek numismatics is normally divided into periods which roughly parallel those established for Greek art in general. The Archaic Period, Classical Period and Hellenistic Period are characterized by stylistic changes which are explained in the following sections. Occasionally one will see references to "the period of finest art" or the period of "the decline of art". These are out-of-date terms used by numismatists and art historians of an earlier generation. They were based on a subjective evaluation of artistic appeal that is invalid—because that appeal changes through time like the swinging of a pendulum. Even the terms Archaic, Classical and Hellenistic are subjective, but they at least do not carry a qualitative implication.

These periods of Greek coinage were not derived from historical, but from artistic developments. Although the beginning and ending dates of each period are tied to an historical event, the basis for each division is really one of artistic style. Over a six hundred year period, Greek art underwent changes which are able to be divided into these three major periods. These were not abrupt changes, and often they evolved during a substantial overlap from one period to the next. Usually, however, the styles are recognizable enough that they fall comfortably into one of these periods. Since the development of style was evolutionary, there are some cases of transitional coins that exhibit tendencies of both the earlier and later period. These are usually quite desirable from a collector's perspective, since they tend to narrow the window of transition and sometimes provide a benchmark for dating or establishing the chronology within a series.

One of the reasons for collecting in general, and for collecting coins in particular, is to satisfy our innate urge to compartmentalize, categorize, label, and organize. Historical events are easily organized and arranged by their chronology. In fact, much has been written about "Historical Greek Coins." Iconography is also studied in the context of one image to another, with topical arrangements providing the means for classification. Thus, the art historian is in many ways like the political or economic historian. The whole concept of "periods" is related to this basic tendency.

Although we are concerned here primarily with Greek coins as works of art, we must acknowledge that not all collectors of this series are inspired by this facet. Metrology is another subject studied in great detail as we classify coins of all periods by composition, size and weight. Political/Geographical relationships are perhaps the most prevalent form of classification, as the majority of coins are described first and foremost by their place of issue or issuing authority. In keeping with our natural habits, we have devised some rather complex methods of classifying and subclassifying coins from the ancient world.

It is only necessary to understand these classifications if one intends to become expert in a particular facet of the hobby. It is not even necessary to understand the differences between Archaic art and Classical art if one simply enjoys the beauty of the object at hand. Inevitably, every collector feels compelled to take that next step toward understanding the broader subject. It is this compulsion that causes us to learn, and to relate one fact to another. So, in the final analysis we find ourselves looking at coins as the product of an age, as voices from the past, and as reflections of a culture that changed from one period to another.

BIBLIOGRAPHY
The Periods of Greek Art

Cook, R.M. *Greek Art, Its Development Character and Influence*, New York, 1972.
Gardner, Percy. *Archaeology and Types of Greek Coins*, London, 1883 (reprint by Argonaut, Chicago, 1965).
Kraay, Colin. *Archaic and Classical Greek Coins*, London, 1976.
Regling, K. *Die antike Münze als Kunstwerk*, Berlin, 1924.
Richter, G.M.A. *The Sculpture and Sculptors of the Greeks*, Yale, 1970.

The Archaic Period

Prior to the eighth century BC sculptural art did not exist in Greece. Painted pottery was geometric in design and the use of figures, much less narrative or allegory, was rare. During that century, however, trade and emigration led to stimulating contacts with the East. By the end of the eighth century, the influence of these contacts was evident. This cultural reflection is generally referred to by art historians as "Orientalizing". Out of this transitional period came the style of art that we refer to as archaic. In fact, some of the coins struck early in the Archaic Period bear floral designs reminiscent of the Orientalizing influence. The Greeks were more free to experiment with new conventions of representation than artists in eastern lands, and they were particularly interested in accurate depiction of the human form.

The Archaic Period—which to art historians began earlier, but for numismatists may be dated approximately from 650 to 479 BC—is marked with important changes in the portrayal of humans. Foremost among these changes, the rigid frontality of eastern sculpture gives way to more flexible profiles. Although the proportions of the human body had not been fully defined, and some of the technical problems of perspective were yet to be resolved, Greek art of the Archaic Period was very innovative. While this style is more fluid than its forerunner, archaic art is still viewed in our minds as "chunky" and "stiff". In comparison to art of the succeeding period it certainly lacks the refinement of the Golden Age.

The concept of *Narrative* in art had evolved in vase painting prior to the invention of coinage. This technique employs multiple images or action to suggest to the viewer a particular theme or emotion. Often, the images used were meaningful in themselves—perhaps from earlier acceptance in another medium. It was natural, therefore, that celators who designed coin motifs incorporated narrative at an early date. For example, the wedding of Peleus and Thetys was a theme of interest to vase painters from the very beginning of narration in art. From this medium, it seems also to have been adapted to numismatic iconography. An electrum stater from Kyzikos, struck about 480 BC, depicts in archaic style a narrative scene very similar to details of the wedding seen on contemporary vases.

Kyzikos, EL stater (x2)
ca. 480 BC

Whether the celator intended to portray a recognizable scene from that mythological tale, or some other oral tradition, it is obvious that the image is narrative in function.

Another mythological allusion (and there are countless other examples which recall narrative traditions) is suggested on an early silver tetradrachm from Potidaia in Macedon. The figure represented on this coin is Poseidon Hippios. We are all

Potidaia, AR tetradrachm ca. 510 BC

aware that Poseidon was the god of the sea, but many are unaware that he also was the divinity who ruled the equine world. On this coin motif he rides at a canter, holding the familiar trident which serves as an attribute. The selection of this particular myth for illustration was probably influenced by a local tradition of horse raising—reflecting a degree of local pride as well as mythological narration.

An early silver drachm from Velia, in Italy, depicts a crouching lion apparently in the act of feeding on its prey. The scene depicts a recognizable act, which probably carries with it a broader meaning. One might say that the difference between portrayal of a standing lion, or lion's head, and this feeding lion

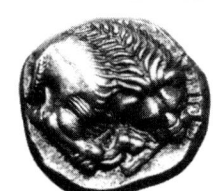

Velia, AR drachm (x2) ca. 500 BC

is like the difference between "See Dick" and "See Dick Run". Not only is this an early example of narrative in art, but also of experimentation with perspective. The lion is presented here in a three-fourths facing position, that is exceptional for the period.

Aside from primitive narration and experimentation with human proportions, one of the hallmarks of the Archaic Period is its beautiful simplicity of form. Earlier, we discussed the interaction between vase painters and celators—in that images were shared by the two. The production of painted pottery in ancient Greece was a collaborative effort of two artists. One created the vase and concerned himself with its shape and form, the other decorated its surface with images. In modern times, we tend to perceive the latter as the more important of the two. But, in ancient times, the potter was equal to the painter in prestige and recognition. Signatures of both often appear on the most elaborate of Attic vases. Form was extremely important in the Greek sense of aesthetics.

Coins of the Archaic Period provide us with wonderful examples of form as an aesthetic virtue. An archaic didrachm from Selinus, on the island of Sicily, bears only a leaf of parsley on its obverse, but what a remarkable leaf it is! Perfectly designed to utilize the circular format of a coin planchet, this punning reference (Parsley= petro**selinon** = rock celery) is so delicately drafted and sensitively modeled that it captures the essence of nature with an extraordinary economy of detail.

Another island coin, a didrachm from Kalymna, bears a lyre—the symbol of Apollo, patron of music and the arts. The simplicity of design here again creates an impression that a mass of detail could not eclipse. Greek art developed from geometric design and the geometry of this design is flawless.

The silver staters from Andros (once attributed as coins of Athens) bear only an amphora on their obverse and the incuse mark of a reverse punch. Andros was celebrated for its wine, and at the time of this coin's issue the motif was probably sufficient for all to recognize its origin. The lack of an inscription may have confused modern day numismatists, but it certainly did not detract from the simplicity of form that these pieces enjoy.

A final example of the geometrically inspired simplicity that graced early Greek coins is seen in a tetradrachm from the city of Eretria. The reverse carries the typical incuse square of archaic issues, but within its confines rests a perfectly symmetrical octopus—of local importance no doubt. This view of nature, as a perfect harmony of curves and lines, is a paradigm of archaic style.

Selinus, Sicily
AR didrachm, ca. 530 BC

Kalymna, Off Caria
AR didrachm, ca. 530 BC

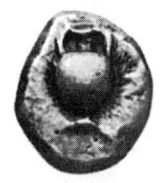

Andros, Cyclades
AR stater, ca. 520 BC

Eretria, Euboia,
AR tetradrachm, ca. 500 BC

Incuse designs on Archaic Greek coins

Among coinage of the late fifth century, an intriguing convention may be seen on coins from Magna Graecia. Obverse designs on these seem typical enough for the time, but the reverses bear incuse images which usually mirror the obverse. On certain types issued jointly by two cities the designs differ, but one is still cameo and the other intaglio. These are not brockages, but were actually struck from reversed image dies. The reason for their inception is unknown. Some numismatists see in them evidence of an early alliance in Magna Graecia.

Sidney Noe *(The Coinage of Metapontum)* discussed the incuse format at some length, but did not offer a plausible reason for its adoption. He did, however, discredit Lenormant's theory that it was a device to facilitate or control trade, and Hill's suggestion that it was a method employed to stack coins more easily. As to the method of production, Noe argued that hubs were used in the production of some types, while hand engraving was employed in others. The reverse designs usually differ slightly from the obverse in their inscriptions, control symbols or ancillary decoration, but some of this could have been added by hand even if a hub were used for die preparation. This "fad" did not last long, but as a result we find an interesting area of specialization for collectors.

KROTON: Delphic Tripod on a silver stater struck about 530 BC

KROTON: Delphic Tripod/Eagle, on a silver nomos (didrachm) struck about 510-480 BC

KROTON and PANDOSIA: Tripod and steer on a silver stater struck about 500 BC

LAOS: Man-headed bull on a silver stater struck about 510 BC

METAPONTUM: Ear of barley on a silver stater struck about 520 BC

METAPONTUM: Ear of barley/Ox head, on a sixth stater, ca. 500 BC

POSEIDONIA: *Poseidon on a silver stater struck about 500 BC*

SYBARIS: *Bull on a silver stater struck about 520 BC*

TARAS: *Phalanthos/dolphin on a silver stater struck about 510 BC*

BIBLIOGRAPHY
The Archaic Period

Gorini, Giovanni. *Le monetazione incusa della Magna Grecia*, Milan, 1975.
Noe, Sidney P. *The Coinage of Metapontum*, ANS, New York, 1984.
Noe, Sidney P. *The Coinage of Caulonia* ANS Numismatic Studies 9, New York, 1958.
Price, Martin and Nancy Waggoner. *Archaic Greek Coinage, The Asyut Hoard*, London 1975.

The Classical Period

The Classical Period starts, by modern consensus, in 479 BC when the Greeks consolidated their efforts to repel the Persian invaders. This is a convenient date to signify the coming of a new age, but artistic style is more often a process of evolution than revolution. The artistic taste of a culture generally changes in a more diffused way. During the Classical Period, mood and feeling became important elements of design, as did the incorporation of allegory and symbolism. Often credited as being the period of finest art in Greece, it is primarily recognized as one of idealism. At this time, Greeks regarded nature as the epitome of perfection, and tried to emulate nature in portraying the ideal human form.

This was the period during which the Parthenon was built and decorated with its magnificent sculpture. It was a period marked by advances in virtually every cultural field, not only at Athens, but in very remote parts of the Greek world. The artists of Magna Graecia working during this period produced masterpieces which have yet to be equalled in 2,500 years of coin production. The fifth century BC was not only a period of great classical achievement, but also one of transition.

There is a marked difference between artistic styles of coinage struck at the beginning of the century and of that struck toward the end. Charles Seltman, in *Approach to Greek Art*, likened the difference to that between poetry and prose. On the Syracusan silver issue referred to by most commentators as the "Demareteion" dekadrachm, Seltman saw a profound example of the former. The work of the celator Kimon, on another dekadrachm struck perhaps 70 years later, was in Seltman's eyes "brilliant prose". The distinctly different emotional effect created by each stylistic treatment is unmistakable.

Demareteion dekadrachm

Kimon dekadrachm

One of the trends which characterize the Classical Period is a steady progression from idealism to naturalism. This trend is readily apparent in images used for the bas-relief sculpture of coinage. Toward the end of the Classical Period, groups and narrative designs start to emerge as coin types.

To many people, the Classical period represents the high point of Greek art. It is hard to deny that images from this period tend to capture the imagination. One characteristic, above all, that seems to permeate this style is the feeling of tension that comes from opposing forces. A great work of classical art can be hard and soft at the same time. It can be inquisitive yet powerful. Facial features may be idealized while hair and adornments are playful. It is often experimental, but not in the sense of the earlier period. Where artists earlier had experimented with poses and perspectives, this new age was different. Artists working at the end of the fifth century are constantly striving for emotional impact. Perhaps one could say that their work was more *spiritual.*

If there is any period in the history of Greek art when the images on coins became models for artists working in other media it was at this time. At the end of the fifth century in Sicily we find virtuosity in celatorship like nothing seen before or since. The imagery on painted pottery, which can usually be dated with a fair degree of accuracy, tends to be inspired by numismatic art at this time. In some cases, scenes are copied with very little deviation. Wonderful chariot scenes that appear on South Italian pottery may consistently be found on earlier coins from Sicily or Magna Graecia. Themes and designs for kylix tondos were also borrowed from the circular motives of coinage. The exchange of ideas between celators, sculptors and painters is not something new to this period, but typically the conservative nature of coin iconography favored the adoption of motives from other disciplines.

Throughout this volume, we have included a great many numismatic works of art from the Classical Period. They are especially to be found in the section about signed dies and in the Masterpieces of Greek Art. It is unnecessary to further illustrate the coins of this period here since all the specimens illustrated elsewhere are dated and are readily identifiable. In our zeal to illustrate the most attractive coins available, we have tended not to illustrate very many bronze coins. This should not be taken as an indication that the bronzes are less appealing. Some of the artists that produced designs for tetradrachms and dekadrachms also designed, and even signed, bronzes during this period. There is something warm in a smooth patination that enhances the appeal of a fine work of art. Perhaps it is that sense of aging that silver coins often lack. A silver coin looks tarnished with age, and if left to the elements long enough becomes almost black. At that point (somewhere beyond the stage we refer to as "old cabinet toning") it loses its appeal. Bronze coins are just the opposite. The hard patina that forms in wonderful browns, greens and black enhances the natural beauty of a coin and makes it a work of art created not only by man but by man and nature.

The Hellenistic Period

The transition from Classical style to Hellenistic style, although more complex than Seltman's analogy of poetry versus prose, can nevertheless be characterized by a similar shift in focus. The prosaic illustration of features is one of the basic tenets of style that characterizes this final period of Greek art.

The accession of Alexander the Great (336 BC) is generally regarded as the beginning of the Hellenistic Period. Politically, this was a period of Greek colonial expansion, and art at the beginning of the period reflects the progressive mind-set of a worldly people. New treatises on proportion (canons) were developed by the leaders of respected schools of art. The most important of these was Lysippos, whose work replaced the venerable canon of Polykleitos. The claim, although probably apocryphal, that Lysippos was the only artist allowed by Alexander to create his image in stone or bronze illustrates nonetheless this artist's tremendous stature. Actually, the fluidity of these new canons is evident somewhat before the accession of Alexander, at an earlier point in the artist's career.

Hellenistic Period posthumous tetradrachm of the "Alexander" style

One of the main differences between art of the Classical period and that of the Hellenistic period is that in the idealism of the former, people were made to look like gods. In the naturalism of the latter, gods were made to look like people. Youthfulness and vibrance replace the idealized perfection of earlier representations. These changes did not occur abruptly, but they become increasingly noticeable on coins struck during the fourth century. The artistic changes of this period parallel a shift in literary conventions. It was at this same time that Xenophon is credited with the birth of biography, and the rise of portraiture is closely related.

As Roman interests in the East and the strength of Roman armies grew, the Hellenist monarchies were hard pressed to respond. Two centuries of infighting had left most of them bankrupt financially and spiritually. Only a few tiny kingdoms survived, and only then as clients of Rome. A logical terminus for the period is the death of Cleopatra VII, the last Hellenistic ruler of Egypt, who committed suicide in 30 BC.

Hellenistic Portraiture

It seems that prior to the death of Alexander the Great it was not considered fashionable among the Greeks for a living ruler to place his or her own portrait on coins. Portraiture had developed in Greece much earlier—for example the sculptor Theodoros cast a self portrait in bronze during the mid 6th century, and we know of portraits of Themistokles and Perikles from the fifth century—but the images on contemporary coins were more conservative. As C.H.V. Sutherland pointed out *(Art in Coinage)*, numismatic art is "... preeminently a social art. The first purpose of coins is to serve as a social commodity—". The use of portraiture as a propagandistic tool did not become commonplace until the Hellenistic Period.

This all changed with the new world view of Greeks that had been to the East with Alexander. It was a time of change in many regards, but not least among them was a new concept of man's place in the universe. One of the main advances characterizing the Hellenistic period was the refinement of naturalistic portraiture, where the recording of individual features became more desirable than the idealized forms of the earlier period. In Hellenistic portraiture the head often turns, twists or looks upward with a fluidity and emotion that Classicism lacks.

Coins were a predictable medium for portraiture, being that subjects were beginning to think of their rulers as individuals rather than esoteric figures. An extensive series of portrait bearing coins from the Hellenistic Period offers the modern day collector a wonderful opportunity to study and enjoy the art and history of this period.

BIBLIOGRAPHY
Hellenistic Portraiture

Curiel, R. and G. Fussmann. *Le trésor monétaire de Qunduz*, Paris, 1965.
Davis, N. and C.M. Kraay. *The Hellenistic Kingdoms: Portrait Coins and History*, London, 1973.
Imhoof-Blumer, F. *Porträtköpfe auf antiken Münzen hellenischer und hellenisierter Völker*, 1885.
Mørkholm, Otto. *Early Hellenistic Coinage from the accession of Alexander to the Peace of Apamea (336-186 B.C.)*. Cambridge, 1991.
Newell, Edward T. *Royal Greek Portrait Coins*, Racine, 1937.
Smith, R.R.R. *Hellenistic Royal Portraits*, Oxford, 1988.
Wace, A.J.B. "Hellenistic Royal Portraits", *Journal of Hellenic Studies* 25, 1905.
Yarkon, Barry. "Kings of Cappadocia struck independent coinage", *The Celator*, Vol. 3 No. 8, August 1989.

Even before the reign of Alexander, there were pockets within the Greek world less bound to the traditional conservatism that avoided portraits. The Persian satrap Pharnabazos is depicted on a tetradrachm from Kyzikos in Mysia struck about 410 BC, and a portrait of the satrap Tissaphernes from Mysia survives on a bronze coin of a few years later. In Lycia, during the period of Persian control, at least three Satraps are known to have placed their likenesses on silver staters. The earliest of these was Kherei, Dynast of Xanthos, who ruled during the last quarter of the 5th century. Following his lead about 380 BC were the dynasts Mithrapata and Perikle of Antiphellos. None of these "portraits" exhibit more than a hint of realism, and understandably so as the Hellenistic style had not fully evolved. Were it not for the fact that the rulers' names accompany these portraits, in lieu of the standard attributes of a deity, we might not recognize them as portraits at all. Although interesting in their own right, these examples do not fall within the normal pattern of Greek art and certainly not within the realm of Hellenistic portraiture. Still, to a portrait collector, they do reflect an early interest in representation of the individual.

The convention of endowing deities or personifications with the physical features of a notable human was thought to have originated early in the fifth century. On the Demareteion dekadrachm (and tetradrachm), it traditionally has been believed that the goddess Arethusa bears some of the features of Queen Demarete. Recent scholarship has proven otherwise, but the fifth century is probably not too early to look for examples of this development.

Pharnabazos, ca. 410 BC
Satrap of Kyzikos

Tissaphernes, ca. 400-395 BC
Satrap of Astyra, Mysia

Kherei, 425-400 BC
Dynast of Xanthos

Dynasts of Antiphellos

Perikle, 380-362 BC

Mithrapata, ca. 380-360 BC

This quasi-portraiture grew in popularity during the fourth century. For example, the facial features of Zeus portrayed on certain coins of Philip II (King of Macedon 359-336 BC) are remarkably similar to those of Philip himself as recorded in contemporary sculpture. Philip's son, Alexander (the Great), undoubtedly allowed his own features to be used in representing Herakles on at least some of the silver tetradrachms struck during his lifetime. The features of Patraos, King of Paeonia, may have inspired at least one variant of the Apollo head on his silver tetradrachms.

This phenomenon continued even after portraits became a common feature on coinage. Early Hellenistic examples include coins struck for Antigonos Gonatas (as Pan), Philip V and his son Perseus (as the hero Perseus) in Macedon, as well as Seleukos I whose depiction of Dionysos on a tetradrachm may reflect the physical features of the Seleukid progenitor. The practice continued throughout the Hellenistic Period. For example, Ptolemy V and Antiochos VI each appear on their coinage as Dionysos. The convention was even adopted by several of the Roman emperors—most notable of these being Nero (strangely enough as Artemis/Diana) and Commodus (as Hercules).

After Alexander's death in 323, his portrait appeared on a number of coins struck in his honor by the successors who divided his empire. Soon, however, they began to place their own portraits on coinage of their independent kingdoms. It was especially common for dynastic rulers to issue portrait coins. Among the most prolific dynasties in this regard were the Antigonid, Seleukid, Ptolemaic, Baktrian and Cappadocian. Lesser dynasties issuing portrait coins include those of Pergamon, Pontos, the Bosporos and Bithynia. In the West,

Philip II as Zeus?
AR tetradrachm
Macedon, 359-336 BC

Patraos as Apollo?
AR tetradrachm,
Paeonia, ca. 335 BC

Philip V as Perseus
AR tetradrachm
Macedon, 221-179 BC

Ptolemy V as Dionysos
AR didrachm, 205-180 BC

only the portraits of Hieron II of Syracuse, and his family, are depicted on coinage. Rulers of Greek lands who owed their sovereignty to the Romans are referred to as Client Kings, and will be discussed in a future volume on Roman Provincial coins. Contemporary Armenian, Parthian and certain other coins which also bear portraits of the issuing authority, are covered in a subsequent volume dealing with the coinage of Nonclassical Cultures.

As might be expected, the portraits found on ancient Greek coins reveal a wide range of styles and varied degrees of draftsmanship. Even within the issues of a particular ruler we are likely to find portraits tending from idealism to verism. The idealized portrait of Hierax (246-227 BC) illustrated here depicts a noble featured young man of flawless physiognomy. From his perfectly coiffured hair to the furrowless brow and hardlined jaw this is a godlike creature. The naturalistic portrait of Hierax leaves quite a different impression. In this case, jowly cheeks and a sagging chin make the subject appear all too human. His deep set eyes lend a certain tension to the portrait that is missing in the idealized version. The more desirable coin to a portrait collector would be the one of naturalistic style.

Idealized Hierax

Naturalistic Hierax

The following section presents a visual guide to those portrait coins struck during the Hellenistic Period by rulers in the Greek lands mentioned above. Only those rulers who struck portrait coins are included, therefore the list is not intended to be complete in any historical sense. The intention here is to illustrate physical features and portrait style, not to record with precision any particular coin. Therefore, illustrations may not conform exactly to the size of the original specimen photographed. The dates used in accompanying descriptions are those proposed by Otto Mørkholm in *Early Hellenistic Coinage*, except for the Baktrian coinage which is dated according to the attributions of O. Bopearachchi in *Monnaies Gréco-Bactriennes et Indo-Grecques*. Many of these dates are the subject of continuing study, debate and controversy and should be considered tentative. The paucity of historical narrative in the Baktrian portrait section is due to the uncertainties of relationships between various rulers resulting from the revisions of dating in recent years. We beg the indulgence of the reader for any confusion resulting from new dates clashing with old interpretations. We have attempted to avoid controversial suggestions.

Alexander the Great

Alexander, the son of Philip II and Olympias, was born into the Temenid dynasty at Pella in 356. The Temenids claimed to be descendent from the Heraclidae of Argos through Temenus, who is said to have founded the kingdom. His father had begun a program of expansion, and had absorbed most of the cities of Greece into the kingdom. It fell to Alexander to carry that program to much greater heights.

Aside from his military prowess, which is legendary, Alexander was a pupil of Aristotle and associated with himself the finest artists in Greece. He understood well the importance of image, and was careful at all times to present an image of invincibility. Although he had his portrait painted by the famous Apelles, and busts in bronze cast by Lysippos, Alexander did not place his portrait directly on his own coins. The portrayal of Herakles certainly takes on the features of Alexander at times, but it is difficult to say how much of that was intention and how much was simply the by-product of idealization.

Hellenistic portraiture really begins with the successors of Alexander the Great, even though earlier isolated examples are known. Immediately following Alexander's death, his portrait appears on coinage of the generals who inherited his kingdom. Shortly thereafter, they placed their own likenesses on their coinage and the practice was followed in most cases by their successors. The image and memory of Alexander persisted into the Roman period, in spite of the tendency toward dynastic portraiture.

by Ptolemy I of Egypt
ca. 315-310 BC

by Seleukos I of Syria
ca. 304-300 BC

by Lysimachos of Thrace
ca. 297-292 BC

Macedon, under the Romans
after 168 BC

Kings of Northern Greece and Asia Minor

MACEDON:

Demetrios Poliorketes, the "Besieger", (294-287 BC): Along with his father, Antigonos Monopthalmos (founder of the Antigonid Dynasty), Demetrios was the first of Alexander's successors to style himself king. Antigonos "The one-eyed" inherited large sections of Asia Minor, and added to it through conquest.

Demetrios Poliorketes

Demetrios won an important victory over Ptolemy I in 306, but his father's kingdom was lost at the Battle of Ipsos in 301. Not to be deterred, Demetrios seized Macedon in 294 and reestablished the dynasty which survived until 168 when it fell to the Romans. Portraits of Demetrios are characterized by the presence of a bull's horn.

Philip V (221-179 BC) was the grandson of Antigonos Gonatas. There do not seem to have been any coins issued by his father, Demetrios II. Philip rose to the throne in 221 on the death of his regent, Doson. His reign was long and successful, but conflict with the Romans left him powerless after the battle of Kynoskephalai. Tetradrachms and minor bronzes bearing the head of the hero Perseus may sometimes reflect the features of Philip.

Philip V

Perseus (179-168 BC) was the final member of the Antigonid Dynasty to rule Macedon. He was named for the hero, from whom his mother was purported to have been descended. The diademed portraits on large flan tetradrachms are of typical Hellenistic style, while representations of the king as the hero Perseus, on bronze coins, are similar to those struck for his father.

Perseus

T. Quinctius Flamininus, (c. 196 BC): the Roman General who defeated Philip V at Kynoskephalai in 197 BC, had his likeness placed on a gold stater issued in Greece. The practice would not have been allowed on a Roman coin, but Flamininus left this Hellenistic portrait for posterity nonetheless.

T. Quinctius Flamininus

THRACE:

Mostis (2nd century BC) was the only Hellenistic king of Thrace to place his portrait on a coin. Specimens are rare and often poorly struck.

Mostis

PERGAMON:

Philetairos, (283-263 BC): Initially appointed by Lysimachos to safeguard the royal treasury of Alexander, Philitairos transferred his loyalties to Seleukos in 282. He declared himself the independent King of Pergamon following the death of Seleukos in 280. Coins bearing the name Philetairos and his portrait were actually struck by his successors Eumenes I and Attalos I. Neither of these rulers placed their own portraits on Pergamene coinage.

Philetairos (by Eumenes I)

Eumenes II (197-158 BC) was the eldest son of Attalos I. He was a loyal ally of the Romans and benefited greatly from that wise choice. The last two Pergamene kings, Attalos II and III, did not strike portrait coins. The kingdom was willed to the Romans in 133 BC and became part of the Roman province of Asia in 130.

Eumenes II

PAPHLAGONIA:

Amastris (300-288 BC) was a niece of Darios III of Persia. She was married at first to the Macedonian general Krateros, then after his death to Dionysos, Tyrant of Herakleia in Bithynia. She was also married for a time to Lysimachos, King of Thrace, who disposed of her to marry Berenike. Finally, she was allowed to found a city on the shores of the Black Sea, which was named after her. She was murdered by her sons in 288.

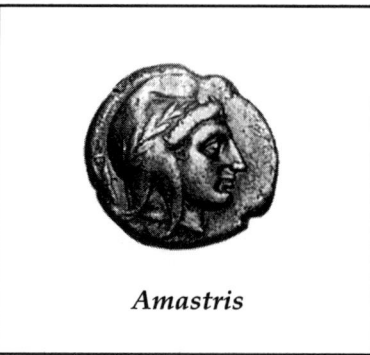

Amastris

Pylaimenes, (ca. 133 BC?): Virtually nothing is known about this king, except that there may be another by the same name at a later date. The king is portrayed here with the attributes of Herakles.

Pylaimenes

PONTOS: (era date = 297 BC)

Mithradates III, (ca. 220 to 185 BC): The fourth in line of succession, was the first Pontic king to place his portrait on a coin. The realism of his features marks these portraits as splendid examples of the Hellenistic style—even though the kings were not themselves of Greek blood.

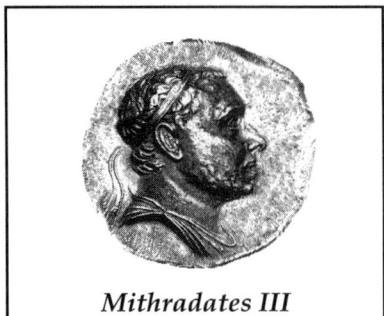
Mithradates III

Pharnakes I, (ca. 185-170 BC): The son of Mithradates III, also placed his portrait on Pontic gold and silver coins. He carried on wars against Pergamon and Cappadociawhich ended in terms of peace unfavorable to Pontos. During his reign of 26 years, the seaport of Sinope was added to the Pontic kingdom and became its capital.

Pharnakes I

Mithradates IV, Philopator, (ca. 170-150 BC): The brother of Pharnakes I established alliances with Rome and Pergamon.

A portrait coin of Mithradates V is known from a single specimen, see Smith, *Hellenistic Royal Portraits*, Plate 77, No, 12.

Mithradates IV

Laodike, (wife of Mithradates IV): Mithradates married his sister and her portrait as Queen appears with his as conjoined busts on a silver tetradrachm. Laodike was the name of the mother of Seleukos I. Several princesses of the Seleukid dynasty bearing this name married into other Hellenistic dynasties and bore daughters also given this name.

Mithradates IV & Laodike

Mithradates VI, Eupator, "The Great", (120-63 BC): This dynamic king came to the throne at the age of eleven. His father was a nephew of Mithradates IV and despite a reign of some 30 years apparently did not issue any coinage in his own name. The son, however, issued one of the most vibrant portrait coins in the Hellenistic series. Mithradates VI was a connoisseur of art, a collector, and was very well educated. As a leader of great prowess, he greatly expanded the Pontic Kingdom and the coinage struck by him, or in recognition of him, is extensive. He inevitably came into conflict with the Romans, and was responsible for the deaths of 80,000 Romans in a single day of mass uprising. A new dating era, established in 88/7 BC when Mithradates first went to war with the Romans, is used on some of the coins struck after that date. His eventual defeat by Pompey the Great, in 63 BC, ended a spectacular reign of 58 years, and a dynastic rule of nearly 240 years.

Mithradates VI

BITHYNIA: (era date = 297 BC)

Nikomedes I, (280-250 BC): Zipoetes I was the first ruler of Bithynia to claim the title King (297/6), but he apparently did not issue any coins. The first portrait coin of this kingdom bears the likeness of his son Nikomedes, who founded the city of Nikomedia.

Ziaelas (250-230 BC) did not issue any silver portrait coins, but his portrait does appear on a very **rare bronze issue—see SNG Von Aulock 243.**

Prusias I, (230-182 BC): The son and successor of Ziaelas issued one of the most attractive portrait coins in the Bithynian series. His rule of 43 years was filled with achievement and prosperity.

Nikomedes I

Prusias I

Prusias II, (182-149 BC): The son of Prusias I was, according to Polybius, an unpopular and weak leader—much less successful than his father. Following an unsuccessful attack on Attalos II of Pergamon, he sacked the Nikephorion stealing the votive statues and cult images of Asklepios. He was overthrown and murdered by his own son Nikomedes II.

Prusias II

Nikomedes II, (149-127 BC): Under his rule, the Bithynian Kingdom was at times allied with Rome, but still maintained a degree of independence. His portrait appears on a gold stater, as well as on silver tetradrachms of his reign. The final rulers of the kingdom, his son Nikomedes III and grandson, Nikomedes IV, retained his portrait on some of their coinage.

Nikomedes II

Nikomedes III, Euergetes, (127-94 BC): The portrait on coins dated to his reign is regarded by some to be that of his father Nikomedes II. This is hardly supported by some of the portraits—which are quite distinctive. We have included here an example of one type which would seem to be a portrait of Nikomedes III.

Nikomedes III

Nikomedes IV, Philopator, (94-74 BC): The coins attributed (by date) to Nikomedes IV have been, like those of his father, attributed as bearing the portrait of Nikomedes II. This seems, on visual evidence alone, not always to be the case.

Nikomedes IV

CAPPADOCIA: (regnal dating)

Ariaramnes, (280-230 BC): The Cappadocian dynasty was founded by Ariarathes I (350-322 BC) who did not issue any portrait coinage. His grandson Ariaramnes was the first of the dynasty to do so, on a small bronze coin of Cappadocia.

Ariaramnes

Ariarathes III, (ca. 230-220 BC): The Cappadocian kings received their recognition from the Seleukid dynasty and maintained close ties with the Seleukids. Ariarathes III married Stratonike, the daughter of Antiochos II. His portrait appears on Cappadocian bronze coins and, according to Newell (Royal Greek Portrait Coins) on a silver tetradrachm which is exceedingly rare.

Ariarathes III

Ariarathes IV, Eusebes, (220-163 BC): The son of Ariarathes III married a daughter of Antiochos the Great but was forced to abandon support of his father-in-law and ally with the Romans. His tetradrachms are scarce, but a large issue of silver drachms was minted—apparently to pay indemnities to Rome.

Ariarathes IV

Ariarathes V, Philopator, (163-130 BC): The son of Ariarathes IV and Antiochis, and a grandson of the Seleukid king Antiochos the Great, was a diplomat and champion of Hellenism. He is considered by some to have been the greatest of Cappadocian kings.

Ariarathes V

Orophernes, (159-157 BC): The portrait of this usurper, who temporarily ruled Cappadocia is one of the finest examples of Hellenistic portraiture in any series. It appears on very rare tetradrachms of his short reign, which are known only from a temple deposit at Priene.

Orophernes

Ariarathes VI, Epiphanes, (130-116 BC): This king acceded the throne as a young boy under the regency of his mother, Queen Nysa. Her portrait is known from a single specimen, with conjoined heads, which is reported in Historia Numorum (Reinach, Trois royaumes, p. 46, no. 14.). Portraits of her son are relatively common on silver drachms.

Ariarathes VI

Ariarathes VII, Philometor, (116-101 BC): The son of Ariarathes VI and Laodike (a daughter of Mithradates V of Pontos) became king upon his father's assassination by a Cappadocian nobleman. Ariarathes VII was subsequently murdered by his uncle, Mithradates the Great, who installed his own son as King of Cappadocia.

Ariarathes VII

Ariarathes VIII, Epiphanes, (101-99 and 90-86 BC): The younger brother of Ariarathes VII ruled for a short time in opposition to the son of Mithradates, but was quickly removed by the Pontic king. He was restored to the throne in 90, with the help of the Romans, but ruled only another four years. With Ariarathes VIII, the Ariarathid Dynasty ended but the coinage of Cappadocia yields additional portraits of succeeding rulers.

Ariarathes VIII

Ariarathes IX, (99-87 BC): Installed at the age of eight by his father, Mithradates VI of Pontos, this young king was eventually deposed by the Romans and died in 87 during the First Mithradatic War. His tetradrachms exhibit a portrait very similar to that of his famous father.

Ariarathes IX

Ariobarzanes I, Philoromaios, (95-63 BC): It was his alliance with the Romans that kept this Cappadocian noble, and successor to the Cappadocian dynasty, in power during a turbulent period. His portrait and those of the remaining kings of the House of Ariobarzanes are found only on silver drachms of a very standard type.

Ariobarzanes I

Ariobarzanes II, Philopator, (63-52 BC): Little is known about the son of Ariobarzanes I despite a reign of more than ten years. He was assassinated by a faction of the court.

Ariobarzanes II

Ariobarzanes III, Eusebes Philoromaios, (52-42 BC): In spite of his surname, which means lover of the Romans, the son of Ariobarzanes II was caught up in the Roman civil wars. He was murdered for refusing aid to Cassius after the assassination of Julius Caesar.

Ariobarzanes III

Ariarathes X, Eusebes Philadelphos, (43-36 BC): The younger brother of Ariobarzanes III. His reign was terminated by Mark Antony who ordered his execution.

Ariarathes X

Archelaos, (36 BC - AD 14): Installed by Mark Antony, this Cappadocian ruler was not of the House of Ariobarzanes. Archelaos was a great-grandson of the general of Mithradates the Great by that same name. He was later confirmed by Augustus and enjoyed a long reign as a Roman Client King.

Archelaos

The Seleukid Dynasty (era date = 312 BC)

Seleukos I, Nikator, (312-281 BC): A close companion of Alexander, Seleukos rose to power in the period of instability following Alexander's death. Although the founder of the Seleukid Dynasty (era dates to 312) did not employ his own portrait on coins struck during his lifetime, tetradrachms struck by Antiochos I and Philetairos bear his portrait.

Seleukos I (by Philetairos)

Antiochos I, Soter, (281-261 BC): The son of Seleukos I reigned jointly with his father in the East from 293 until 280, when he inherited the Seleukid throne. He overcame numerous challenges, including a Gallic invasion of Asia Minor (which earned him the name Soter—"Savior"). He died at Sardeis in Lydia.

Antiochos I

Antiochos II, Theos, (261-246 BC): The son of Antiochos I and Stratonike was a weak ruler who lost substantial lands in the East—particularly the regions of Baktria which fell to the rebel Diodotos, and Parthia which fell to Arsakes. He divorced Laodike, and took Berenike (the daughter of Ptolemy) as his second wife—subsequently being murdered, according to rumor, by the former.

Antiochos II

Seleukos II, Kallinikos, (246-226 BC): This elder son of Antiochos II spent a troubled reign in conflict with his brother Hierax. His portrait appears in all metals, sometimes clean-shaven and sometimes bearded.

Seleukos II

Antiochos Hierax (246-226 BC): Temporarily co-regent, Hierax was deposed by his brother Seleukos II. Thereafter, he ruled independently in Asia Minor with the help of his mother Laodike. He unsuccessfully tried to expand into his brother's lands, and finally was murdered during a Gallic excursion into the region.

Antiochos Hierax

Seleukos III, Soter, Keraunos, (226-223 BC): The elder son of Seleukos II, and brother of Antiochos III, led a failed campaign against Pergamon and was murdered by his own officers.

Seleukos III

Antiochos III, the Great, (223-187 BC): Succeeding his brother while only a teenager, this king proved to be one of the greatest leaders of the Seleukid dynasty. He regained much of the land lost by his predecessors, but was defeated twice by the Romans, losing most of Asia Minor after his defeat at Magnesia in 190. He was eventually murdered on an eastern campaign.

Antiochos III

Achaios, (220-213 BC): The uncle of Antiochos III was appointed by his nephew to govern Asia Minor, but rebelled and was beheaded following a two-year siege of his stronghold at Sardeis in Lydia. His portrait is found only on a unique gold coin and on rare silver tetradrachms.

Achaios

Seleukos IV, Philopator, (187-175 BC): The son of Antiochos III inherited a weakened kingdom, drained by huge war indemnities, but managed well until he was murdered by his minister Heliodoros.

Seleukos IV

Antiochos, (c. 175-170 BC): The son of Seleukos IV was only five years old when his father was murdered. Heliodoros assumed power in the name of the young prince as regent but was displaced by a brother of Seleukos IV (also named Antiochos) who had been hostage in Rome. For a short time, the young Antiochos was affiliated with his uncle of the same name as joint ruler. After 170 BC nothing more is heard of him.

Antiochos

Antiochos IV, Epiphanes (175-164 BC): The younger son of Antiochos III deposed the regent Heliodoros, but is perhaps best known for tearing down the city wall of Jerusalem and desecrating the Temple of the Jews. He was an adventurer, extravagant in his life-style, who died on an expedition into Persia.

Antiochos IV

Antiochos V, Eupator, (164-162 BC): Eupator was co-regent with his father Antiochos IV in 165, but was placed under the regency of Lysias on his father's death. The nine year old was barely established on the Seleukid throne when he fell victim to his murdering cousin Demetrios I.

Antiochos V

137

Demetrios I, Soter, (162-150 BC): The elder son of Seleukos IV was a hostage at Rome when his father died and younger brother was elevated under the regency of Heliodoros. He eventually escaped from Rome and reclaimed the Seleukid throne, only to die in battle against the claimant Alexander Balas.

Demetrios I

Laodike, (Wife and sister of Demetrios I): The widow of Perseus, King of Macedon, appears with her brother/husband on silver and bronze coins bearing conjoined heads.

Demetrios and Laodike

Timarchos, (162-160 BC): This usurper in Babylon refused to accept Demetrios I as king in the newly conquered lands and established himself as King of Media. The rebellion was crushed by Demetrios.

Timarchos

Alexander I Balas, (150-145 BC): Gaining power in Syria through the help of Pergamene and Ptolemaic rulers, Alexander ruled five years, apparently in a life-style of excess, before he was defeated by Demetrios II and murdered while fleeing Antioch.

Alexander I, Balas

Demetrios II, Nikator, (145-140 BC and 129-125 BC): The elder son of Demetrios I overthrew Alexander Balas, but was later captured by the Parthians where he was held in captivity for 10 years. He was released in 129, and resumed his position as Seleukid King but was murdered at Tyre in 125. His portrait appears both bearded and unbearded on silver and bronze coins.

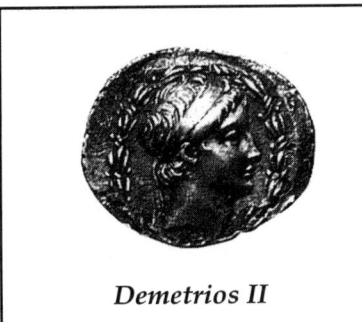

Demetrios II

Antiochos VI, Dionysos, (145-142 BC): Following the death of Alexander Balas, his infant son was proclaimed king by a rebel general named Diodotos. Coins with the young king's portrait were struck in relatively large numbers at Antioch.

Antiochos VI

Tryphon, (142-138? BC): The general Diodotos (not a Seleukid) murdered the young Antiochos VI, whom he had earlier elevated to the throne, and proclaimed himself king under the name Tryphon. His usurpation was temporarily successful due to the internal turmoil of the time.

Tryphon

Antiochos VII, Sidetes, Euergetes, (138-129 BC): The younger brother of Demetrios II succeeded his brother after the latter's capture by the Parthians and ruled with great skill. He deposed Tryphon, and embarked on a campaign to recover lost Seleukid lands, but was killed in battle against the Parthians in 129 BC.

Antiochos VII

Alexander II, Zebina, (128-123 BC): The supposedly adopted son of Alexander Balas rebelled against Demetrios II and following a victory at Damaskos held a position of power for five years. His portrait is common in all metals except gold, where it is known from a unique specimen.

Alexander II, Zebina

Cleopatra Thea, (125 BC): The daughter of Ptolemy VI married Alexander Balas, Demetrios II and Antiochos VII in succession before assuming the Seleukid throne in her own name. This she did by disposing of her own son, Seleukos V (no coins known). Her portrait alone appears on a rare silver tetradrachm; and also conjoined with that of her son Antiochos VIII on silver and bronze coins of lesser rarity.

Cleopatra Thea and Grypos

Antiochos VIII, Grypos, (126-96 BC): In a fair-play turnabout, Antiochos disposed of his ambitious mother by forcing her to drink a cup of poison she had prepared for him. He then ruled in his own name for 25 years. Although enjoying a long term, by standards of the time, his leadership was not exceptional. Coins of this ruler bear the epithet "Epiphanes." He was murdered in 96.

Antiochos VIII Grypos

Antiochos IX, Philopator, Kyzikenos, (114-95 BC): The son of Antiochos VII and Cleopatra captured Antioch in 113 and carved out a position of power in opposition to his half-brother Antiochos VIII, surviving him by a single year before falling victim in a campaign against Seleukos VI.

Antiochos IX

Seleukos VI, Epiphanes Nikator, (95 BC): The eldest son of Antiochos VIII ruled at Antioch for a very short time after defeating Antiochos IX (an uncle) and succumbing to Antiochos X (a cousin) at Mopsos in Cilicia. Despite the short reign, coins of this ruler are not exceedingly rare.

Seleukos VI

Antiochos X, Eusebes Philopator, (95 BC): The son of Antiochos IX defeated Seleukos VI to regain the throne for his family. His reign was marked by internal family wars.

Antiochos X

Antiochos XI, Philadelphos, (95-84 BC): A son of Antiochos VIII, this claimant lost his life in battle with Antiochos X. He apparently drowned while trying to flee across the Orontes.

Antiochos XI

Demetrios III, Philopator (95-88 BC): Also a son of Antiochos VIII, this claimant secured a power base at Damaskos and with the help of his brother Philip defeated Antiochos X. He later was defeated by Philip as the brothers contended for power.

Demetrios III

Philip, Philadelphos, (95-84 BC): Another son of Antiochos VIII, Philip was burdened with wars within the family. His portrait in silver is very common and rather unexceptional. Tetradrachms bearing his portrait were also struck under Roman authority after 64 BC.

Philip, Philadelphos

Antiochos XII, Dionysos, (87-84 BC): The youngest son of Antiochos VIII succeeded Demetrios III, but failed to gain further lands under the control of his brother Philip. He was killed in an excursion against the Nabataeans. His silver tetradrachms are rare, but a portrait in bronze is also obtainable.

Antiochos XII

Antiochos XIII, Asiatikos, (69-68 and 65-64 BC): Pompey the Great organized Syria as a Roman province in 64 BC and retained the son of Antiochos X as a Roman client king. Murdered shortly thereafter by an Arab Emir, he was the last of the Seleukid dynasty to rule in Syria.

Antiochos XIII

BIBLIOGRAPHY
The Seleukid Dynasty

Newell, Edward T. *The Seleucid Mint of Antioch*, 1917, (reprint, Chicago, 1978).
_____ *The Coinage of the Eastern Seleucid Mints, from Seleucos I to Antiochus III*, New York, 1938.
_____ *The Coinage of the Western Seleucid Mints, from Seleucus I to Antiochus III*, New York, 1941.
Houghton, A. *Coins of the Seleucid Empire from the Collection of Arthur Houghton*, ANS, New York, 1983.

The Ptolemaic Dynasty (regnal dating)

Ptolemy I, Soter, (305-283 BC): As a trusted general and lifelong friend of Alexander, Ptolemy inherited Egypt where he founded a dynasty (the Lagids = Ptolemy, son of Lagos) that lasted almost three centuries. His biography of Alexander (known to us through Arrian) is the source for much of what we know today about the great conqueror. Ptolemy declared himself King of Egypt in 305 and immediately placed his own portrait on the coinage.

Ptolemy I

Berenike I, (Wife of Ptolemy I): Berenike literally means "bearer of Victory". Before becoming the wife of Ptolemy she was married to another Macedonian by the name of Philip and had children including Magas, the King of Kyrene.

Ptolemy I and Berenike I

Ptolemy II, Philadelphos, (285-246 BC): The son of Ptolemy I, ruled jointly with his father for two years. He married first Arsinoe I, the daughter of Lysimachos and then his own sister Arsinoe II. During his reign the Lighthouse and Library of Alexandria were built.

Ptolemy II & Arsinoe II

Arsinoe II, (died 270 BC): This daughter of Ptolemy I and Berenike was once the wife of Lysimachos of Thrace. On his death, she married her stepbrother Ptolemy Keraunos, but was quickly exiled to Samothrace. About 276 she married her natural brother Ptolemy II and became the real power behind the throne in Egypt.

Arsinoe II

Ptolemy III, Euergetes, (246-222 BC): The strong and bellicose son of Ptolemy II and Arsinoe I (daughter of Lysimachos) avenged the murder of his sister and extended the Ptolemaic Kingdom into Cilicia and beyond Syria—making Egypt a major power.

Ptolemy III

Berenike II: The daughter of Magas of Kyrene, and granddaughter of Antiochos I of Syria, married Ptolemy III and ruled in his absence while he campaigned in Syria. She was not only beautiful, but blessed with extraordinary strengths and virtues.

Berenike II

Ptolemy IV, Philopator, (222-205 BC): The son of Ptolemy III and Berenike II. A ruler without character or distinction was married to his sister Arsinoe III. Newell refers to him as a "sot and a soft voluptuary", Polybius as a "scoundrel". His reign was marked by the loss of much that had been achieved before him.

Ptolemy IV

Arsinoe III: The sister and wife of Ptolemy IV, she was murdered following the mysterious death of her brother.

Arsinoe III

Ptolemy V, Epiphanes, (205-180 BC): The son of Ptolemy IV and Arsinoe III, only five years old at his father's death, was elevated under the regency of Sosibios, one of the conspirators who murdered his parents. The conspirators were subsequently removed by an uprising of the populace. Epiphanes died at 29.

Ptolemy V

Cleopatra I, (died 176 BC): The daughter of Antiochos III of Syria became the wife of Ptolemy V—to whom she bore two boys and a girl.

Cleopatra I

Ptolemy VI, Philometor, (180-145 BC): The son of Ptolemy V and Cleopatra I was under the regency of his mother until her death. He married his sister, Cleopatra II. Philometor died in a campaign against Alexander Balas of Syria, having made his young son Ptolemy VII (Neos Philopator) joint ruler. The son survived only one year as sole ruler and did not issue any portrait coins.

Ptolemy VI

Ptolemy VIII, Euergetes, (164-163 and 145-116 BC): A son of Ptolemy V and Cleopatra I. He ruled jointly with his older brother Ptolemy VI from 164 to 163 BC and was then deposed to Kyrenaica. After the death of Ptolemy VI he reclaimed the throne of Egypt, married his sister Cleopatra II, and murdered his nephew Ptolemy VII. He then took a second wife, Cleopatra

Ptolemy VIII

III, the daughter of his first wife and Ptolemy VI (his older brother). His two sons by Cleopatra III (Ptolemy IX and X) and his grandson Ptolemy XI ruled Egypt from 116-80 BC. The portrait on their coins is universally attributed as that of Ptolemy I—although there are significantly differing features within the series, some of which may someday be proven to be portraits of these kings.

Ptolemy XII, Neos Dionysos, (80-58 and 55-51 BC): The illegitimate son of Ptolemy IX, fled Egypt on the death of his father, but was recalled to replace Ptolemy XI. He proved unpopular and was deposed in 58, but regained his crown through the help of the Romans. He died in 51. His portrait appears on a silver tetradrachm of Askalon and on a drachm of Alexandria.

Ptolemy XII

Cleopatra VII, Philopator, (51-30 BC): This daughter of Ptolemy XII and Cleopatra VI was the captivating and impetuous "Queen of the Nile", of historical fame. She committed suicide following Octavian's capture of Alexandria in 30 BC. This brought to an end the Ptolemaic dynasty in Egypt, although the children of Cleopatra and Antony survived. Her daughter, Cleopatra Selene, married Juba II (a Roman Client King) and became Queen of Mauretania. They had a son named Ptolemy who ruled Mauretania for quite a long time after the death of his father.

Cleopatra VII

The Baktrian Kings

The history of Baktria is very poorly recorded, and even dates of reign are difficult to determine. The following dates and attributions must be considered tentative.

Diodotos I, Soter, (ca. 250-230 BC): Diodotos served under Antiochos II, Seleukid king of Syria, as Satrap of Baktria/Sogdiana. He rebelled sometime between 256 and 250 and established himself as independent ruler of the region. The dates of rule in this series are not entirely certain, and are therefore given as approximate.

Diodotos I

Diodotos II, Theos, (ca. 250-230 BC) : According to Justin, the son of Diodotos I ruled jointly with his father as satrap and king until the latter's death. The assignment of coins to Diodotos I and II is controversial and is very often based on variations in portraiture.

Diodotos II

Euthydemos I (ca. 230-200 BC) deposed Diodotos about 230 BC and assumed the throne of Baktria-Sogdiana. During his reign he was defeated in battle by Antiochos III of Syria, and also lost the district of Sogdiana to rebels. He did manage to hold the city of Balkh and a semblance of independence.

Euthydemos I

Demetrios I, (ca. 200-190 BC) : The son of Euthydemos I was associated with his father as ruler from about 205 until the death of Euthydemos in 200. From that point he ruled in his own name and associated with him his own son Euthydemos II. He expanded the Baktrian Kingdom into the northern frontiers of India.

Demetrios I

Euthydemos II, (ca. 190-185 BC): This ruler seems to have been the eldest son of Demetrios I, and grandson of Euthydemos I. Based on stylistic similarities seen in their coinage, Bopearachchi suggests that he was associated with Agathokles and Pantaleon. He apparently ruled in the southern regions of the kingdom.

Euthydemos II

Agathokles, (ca. 190-180 BC) : Perhaps a son of Demetrios, Agathokles ruled with Euthydemos II—and may have been a brother of Pantaleon. He ruled in that part of the kingdom south of the Hindu Kush that was taken from India. Some of his coins include Brahmi inscriptions.

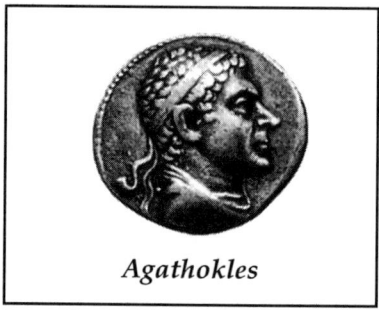
Agathokles

Pantaleon, (ca. 190-185 BC): Ostensibly a second son of Demetrios, Pantaleon was associated with his uncle and his brother, (or as the case may be, two other brothers) as joint ruler. He also ruled in the area of Baktrian expansion to the south.

Antimachos I, Theos, (ca. 185-170 BC): Upon the death of Euthydemos II, Antimachos (perhaps a brother of Demetrios) became the main ruler of the kingdom while Agathokles ruled to the south. He also struck coins bearing the portrait of Diodotos, to bolster his dynastic legitimacy.

Pantaleon

Apollodotos I, (ca. 180-169 BC): This associate of Antimachos I, who succeeded Agathokles in the south, struck minor coins with Indian motifs and bilingual (Greek/Karosthi)

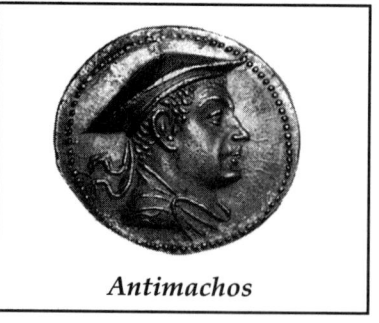
Antimachos

inscriptions, his portrait is known only from a rare type found at Aï Khanoum (see Bopearachchi plate 11, 1A). His successor, Antimachos II, did not issue portrait coins.

Demetrios II, (ca. 175-170 BC): The coins of this ruler are distinguished from those of (his father?) Demetrios I by their style. The identification of this king and his placement in the chronology of rulers eliminates a dating disparity between the revolt of Eukratides and the death of the earlier Demetrios.

Demetrios II

Eukratides I, (ca. 170-145 BC): Rising to power through revolt, Eukratides established a stable and prosperous kingdom following the disposition of Demetrios II. He appointed Sub-kings to rule parts of his domain, but struck coins with both unilingual and bilingual legends. The latter for use in southern regions of the kingdom. Some of his tetradrachms are superb examples of Hellenistic portraiture at its best.

Eukratides I

Heliokles and Laodike, (father and mother of Eukratides I): These family portraits were presumably placed on the reverse of a portrait coin of Eukratides to bolster recognition of his pedigree, and improve his perceived legitimacy in the face of a bold usurpation.

Heliokles and Laodike

Eukratides II, (ca. 145-140 BC): This successor of Eukratides I, presumably a son, has been a subject of lengthy debate. Whether there are actually two kings by that name is far from certain. Bopearachchi assigns the portraits of this type to Eukratides II, and ties them stylistically to the coins of Plato and Heliokles I.

Eukratides II

Plato, (ca. 145-140 BC): Apparently Plato was appointed co-ruler by Eukratides I, but did not issue coins in his own name until his superior's death. The coins of Plato, Eukratides and Heliokles I are seen by Bopearachchi as contemporary due to their similarities of iconography and fabric.

Plato

Heliokles I, (ca. 145-130 BC): It is said that Heliokles became the ruler of Baktria by murdering his father Eukratides. He thereafter shared the kingdom with Eukratides II, who would seem to be his brother. He lost most of his kingdom, however, to Skythian invaders.

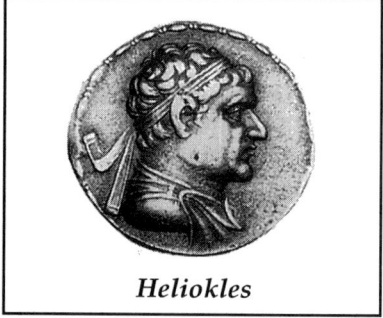
Heliokles

Menander, Soter, (ca. 155-130 BC): Associated as king with Eukratides I, Menander became one of the most historically famous of the Indo-Greek rulers. Strabo recounted that he conquered more of India than Alexander the Great. His popularity, and the immense quantity of coins issued in his name, have secured his place in history.

Menander

Strato I, (ca. 130-110 BC): The son of Menander ruled under the regency of his mother Agathokleia until 125, and from then in his own right. His coinage, which was copious, tends to repeat the types of his father. Prior to her son's attainment of majority, Agathokleia also issued coins with her portrait alone. After 125, Strato appears alone on portrait coins.

Strato and Agathokleia

Zoilos I, (ca. 130-120 BC): Following the death of Menander, Zoilos appears to have shared the reign with Agathokleia and Strato for a time. Although most of his coins are bilingual, they are characterized by a return of Greek iconography in various representations of Herakles.

Zoilos I

Lysias, (ca. 120-110 BC): Based on the evidence of repeating monograms, Lysias seems to have taken or been awarded control of certain parts of the kingdom of Strato. It is also clear from the analysis of these monograms that Lysias and Antialkidas were associated in the same region that Zoilos ruled.

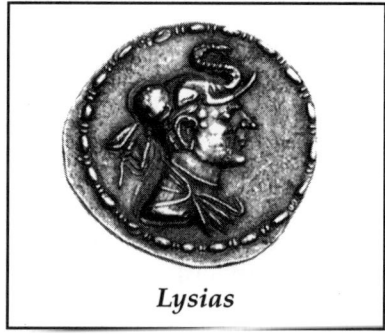

Lysias

Antialkidas, (ca. 115-95 BC): From 115, Antialkidas was associated with Lysias—apparently in the southern regions of Baktria—and issued an extensive series of silver and bronze coins. The monograms on coins of Antialkidas repeat exactly those on the coins of Lysias, while those of Strato are repeated on coins of Heliokles II. This seems to confirm the alignment of king and sub-king by region.

Antialkidas

Heliokles II, (ca. 110-100 BC): As stated above, Heliokles II seems to have been a successor to Strato. This ruler is distinguished from the former Heliokles by physiognomy, fabric of the issues, and the incorporation of bilingual inscriptions on the reverses of this later ruler. By the end of his reign, he seems to have reached a position of equality with Antialkidas.

Heliokles II

Polyxenos, (ca. 100-95 BC): Based on monogram analysis, Polyxenos seems to have succeeded Heliokles II. His coins are rare and portrait coins are exceedingly so. The reverse of his silver coins copies the earlier type of Athena Alkidemos, protectress of the city, issued by Menander and Strato I.

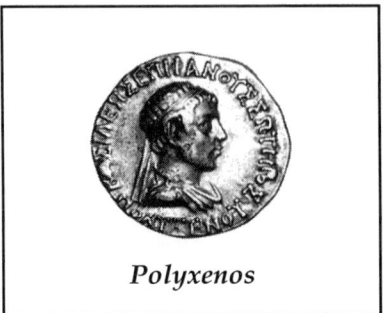
Polyxenos

Demetrios III, Aniketos, (ca. 100 BC): This ruler was first identified in 1981 by C.M. Kraay. He was apparently a contemporary of Antialkidas, but only for a very short time. The unique specimen illustrated here was published in 1923 by R.B. Whitehead as an example of overlapping standards within the reign of Demetrios I.

Demetrios III

Philoxenos, (ca. 100-95 BC): Another contemporary of Antialkidas, this sub-king seems to have been a successor to parts of the region ruled by Heliokles II. Based on the substance of his coinage, both in quality of celatorship and variety of types, it must be assumed that his short reign was relatively prosperous.

Philoxenos

Diomedes, (ca. 95-90 BC): It is fairly clear, as least as clear as any relationships in this series can be, that Diomedes was a successor to Philoxenos in the lands formerly ruled by Heliokles II. The predominant motif on the reverses of coins issued by this king are the Dioscouri, standing and on horseback. Although his coins are scarce, the diversity is fairly broad.

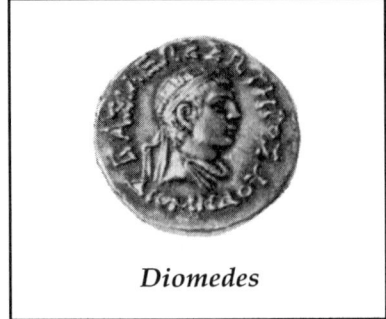
Diomedes

Amyntas, (ca. 95-90 BC): The

dates assigned here are based on the studies and arguments of Osmund Bopearachchi, which we have accepted for the purpose of this introduction and portrait list. Amyntas precedes Archebios and Hermaios in this study. The most remarkable occurrence in the coinage of Amyntas was the issue of double dekadrachms of two types, discovered in the "Qunduz Treasure".

Amyntas

Epander, (ca. 95-90 BC): The period from 95 to 85 BC is extremely cloudy in terms of which rulers controlled various parts of a fragmented kingdom. The report of an overstruck bronze coin with the overtype of Epander and the undertype of Philoxenos places this ruler later in the sequence.

Epander

Theophilos, (ca. 90 BC): The coinage of Theophilos is not only rare, it is remarkable for its iconography. The reverse motif of silver coins in this reign boasts Athena Nikephoros, a victory allusion. This motif is unique to the series except for a single type of Apollodotos I. He also adopts the title "Autokrator" which exceptional.

Theophilos

Peukolaos, (ca. 90 BC): The rarity of issues struck by this king, and the short term of his reign, coupled with the lack of historical evidence, make any comments at all conjectural. We know many of these kings only from the names and faces on their surviving coins. Still, one cannot help but appreciate the amount of knowledge that has been gleaned in the past century.

Peukolaos

Nikias, (ca. 90-85 BC): Along with Theophilos, Peukolaos and Artemidoros, this king ruled part of the region of Gandhara in northwest India. His coins, although issued in both silver and bronze, are rare. Aside from minor legend variations, they are typical for the period—with bilingual inscriptions and Greek deities as reverse motifs.

Nikias

Menander II, Dikaios, (ca. 90-85 BC): The coins of this ruler have often been attributed to the reign of Menander I, Soter, or his son. The fabric and style do not allow such an interpretation however, and the coins of Menander Dikaios have now been assigned to this later period. Like the coins of other petty kings of this period, they are very rare.

Menander II, Dikaios

Artemidoros, (ca. 85 BC): A standing figure of the goddess Artemis was employed as a tutelary deity on some of this ruler's coins. It was more likely a pun on the king's name than any serious form of reverence to Artemis. Nike also appears as a motif on silver coins, and the "Brahmin" bull on bronzes.

Artemidoros

Archebios, (ca. 90-80 BC): Due to their short reigns and transitory nature, Bopearachchi refers to Diomedes through Archebios as "Ephemeral Kings". Archebios was the last Greek king to reign at Taxila before the Indo-Skythian invasion of Maues. His coinage was the most extensive of all these ephemeral kings and includes some fairly realistic portraits.

Archebios

Hermaios. (ca. 90-70 BC): Long thought to be the last king of the Indo-Greeks, Hermaios has now been assigned an earlier date. His coinage is extensive and a long series of posthumous issues bearing his name has added greatly to confusion about his dates of reign. The posthumous coins quickly deteriorate in style and quality.

Hermaios

Kalliope, (wife of Hermaios): She was associated with her husband early in his reign and appears with him as conjoined busts on silver drachms and tetradrachms.

Hermaios and Kalliope

Apollodotos II, (ca. 80-65 BC): Following the Indo-Skythian invasion and the ten year domination of Maues, a few Greek rulers managed to reconsolidate their power. Among these was Apollodotos II, who can be considered one of the most important Greek kings after Menander Soter. His coinage reflects a revival of power and prosperity—for a time at least.

Apollodotos II

Hippostratos, (ca. 65-55 BC): This successor to Apollodotos also produced an extensive and impressive series of coins. He included the epithet Soter (savior) on several types, and included a variety of Greek deity reverses. The quality of engraving and striking suggests a reign of some stability. All of his coins are bilingual.

Hippostratos

Dionysios, (ca. 65-55 BC): The coinage of Dionysios lacks any semblance of the character seen in coins of his contemporary Hippostratos. Portraits are known only from a few rare drachms, which have not been bolstered by the hoard finds of recent years. His power base was obviously much more restricted than that of Hippostratos.

Dionysios

Zoilos II, (ca. 55-35 BC): There does not seem to be any connection between this king and the earlier Zoilos I. There certainly can be no confusion about which ruler the coins should be assigned to. Portraits of this king are extremely crude, and the coins themselves are poorly manufactured, with flans that seldom accommodate the full die.

Zoilos II

Apollophanes, (ca. 35-25 BC): There are not many coins known of this king, and all of them are from the same mint workshop. Portraits during this period have become meaningless as individual representations and only signify the abstract concept of kingship.

Apollophanes

Strato II, (ca. 25 BC - AD 10): This king was the last Indo-Greek ruler in the East. Although his coins still proclaim the king as savior, it must have been a very hollow promise at this point, with a very small toehold in an isolated corner of the world. In his final days, Strato II associated his son with him as king of the Indo-Greeks.

Strato II

Family of Hieron II

Hieron II, (275-215 BC): This wise and popular ruler was the first Greek tyrant to openly place his image on coins of the realm. Rising from a humble beginning, Hieron became the leader of the army and married the beautiful aristocrat Philistis. He was acknowledged as King of Syracuse by the will of the people.

Hieron II

Philistis, (Wife of Hieron II): The daughter of Leptines, descended from a brother of Dionysios the Elder, gave Hieron a measure of noble respectability and acceptance in Syracusan society. She appears veiled, in the guise of Demeter, on coins of Hieron's reign.

Philistis

Gelon, (Son of Hieron): The Syracusan heir presumptive died shortly before his aged father, but his portrait appears on silver coins of his father's reign.

Gelon

Hieronymos, (215-214 BC): The second son of Hieron ascended the throne at the age of 15. He was unequal to the task in every respect and was soon assassinated. The ensuing siege of Syracuse ended in 212 with the fall of the city to the Romans.

Hieronymos

MASTERPIECES OF GREEK ART

The following pages present a kaleidoscope of Greek numismatic art from the Archaic Period through the Hellenistic Period. All of the coins chosen for this section have been sold in the trade within the past twenty years. They represent the author's personal and subjective opinion as to quality and suitability for the accolade "Masterpiece". There have been many other beautiful coins sold during this period, some even more beautiful than those featured here, but this is not a "Who's Who" of ancient numismatics. It is a pleasing collection of images that illustrate the author's thesis.

The dies which produced these coins must, above all, have been designed and engraved with extraordinary skill. They must reflect the highest level of excellence within the period and style of consideration. They are not all expensive coins, at least not relatively so. We hope they will graphically illustrate the trite but true adage that Greek coins are exceptional works of art—or at least *can* be.

Masterpieces of Greek Art

Kaulonia, AR stater, ca. 520 BC

This stater from Kaulonia perfectly exemplifies the archaic style. The simplified and exaggerated musculature, ringlets of hair, twisted torso and rigid stance are characteristic of early attempts to render the human form. Distinctive facial features include a pronounced angular nose and jaw, frontal oval eye, and "archaic smile". In this composition Apollo holds a laurel branch in his right hand while a miniature naked figure, also carrying a branch, is borne running on his outstretched left arm. In the field to the right is a stag, and to the left the abbreviated ethnic KAVΛ for Kaulonia. Both Apollo and the stag are set on a baseline. In spite of the early nature of this composition, the artist's interest in perspective and adaptation to the circular space are obvious.

Masterpieces of Greek Art

Kyzikos, EL stater, ca. 480 BC

The imagery on this electrum stater from Kyzikos is straightforward enough. The head of a male goat faces left, with the obligatory tunny fish in the field to the right. The tunny was a heraldic symbol of Kyzikos and it appears (unfortunately) on virtually all of their electrum coins. It seldom, if ever, becomes a part of the motif—only a politically necessitated appendage. The denomination circulated widely, and some stamp of assurance was indispensable. At least, the artist has tried to hide it in the least conspicuous spot. The goat is most likely a reference to Dionysos, for whom the animal is sacred. The main divinity at Kyzikos was Persephone, who is very closely related to Dionysos in a variety of mythological traditions. Other staters from this city also bear Dionysiac allusions.

A remarkably detailed beard and deeply modelled facial features mark this die as the work of a master engraver. It is unusually faithful to nature for such an early work, and is all the more exceptional considering that the coin itself is only about 1/2 inch in diameter. Three innocent folds on the neck help the image to effortlessly conjure up a sense of determination and strength. At the same time, it retains a delightful simplicity through reliance on form and economy of line.

Masterpieces of Greek Art

Syracuse, AR dekadrachm, ca. 465 BC

The "Demareteion" dekadrachm is one of the most famous and beautiful of all Greek coins. It was Sicily's first 10 drachm coin, and was struck at the same time that Pheidias was completing his Parthenon sculptures in Athens. It is a wonderful example of early classical art. The name by which we know this piece comes from a romantic, but unfortunately inaccurate, tradition. Since the 19th century it has been believed that this coin was produced from a gift to Queen Demarete, the wife of Gelon. Demarete is said to have interceded for the Carthaginians after their loss to the Greeks in 480 BC. They rewarded her with an immensely valuable diadem, which was supposedly used to mint these dekadrachms.

The artist who designed this motif is unknown by name, but is commonly called the "Demareteion Master". He also produced tetradrachms for Syracuse and Leontini. It was suggested that the features of Arethusa on this issue were actually those of the queen, but modern scholarship has negated this connection. Nevertheless, these coins will probably always be called Demareteion dekadrachms, and after all, a rose is a rose.

Masterpieces of Greek Art

Selinus, AR tetradrachm, ca. 460 BC

This early classical composition, centered around the river god Selinus, is clearly narrative—but what story do all of the elements combine to tell? The intrigue is enhanced by a similar and contemporary motif which portrays the river god Hypsas, also sacrificing at an altar (the Selinus and Hypsas were local rivers). They differ in one notable respect, the "Selinus" variety includes a cock and the statue of a bull in the iconography while the "Hypsas" variety substitutes a snake and a stork in the same roles. Percy Gardner *(Archaeology and Types of Greek Coins)* proposed an interesting answer, for which he credits Müller and Lloyd. "It would appear that....these representations contain allusions to the same event, the draining of some marshes at Selinus by the well-known philosopher Empedocles, whereby health was given to the district and freshness to the waters of its streams. Selinus and Hypsas sacrifice in thanksgiving....the cock and snake are alike symbols of the god of healing and cleansing, Asklepios; while the marsh bird, the stork, is retiring because the marshes wherein he used to feed are no more." Alan Walker submits that the statue of the bull, which is heretofore unexplained, may represent the "wild" river god, which can only be remembered monumentally now that the river is tamed.

Masterpieces of Greek Art

Naxos, AR tetradrachm, ca. 460 BC

One of the most famous engravers of the fifth century in Sicily is known to us not by name, but by a modern designation "The Aitna Master". His career reached its apogee between 470 and 460 BC as he produced masterful dies for the cities of Aitna (Katana) and Naxos. The Aitna Master derived inspiration from Athenian vase painters, but his virtuosity in the three dimensional medium of coinage far exceeded that of his Athenian colleagues. The squatting satyr Silenus is derived from the Dionysiac iconography of Greek mythology. In some accounts, he was the foster-father of the infant Dionysos. He is usually depicted with Dionysiac accoutrements like a wine skin and grape leaves or ivy. On the coin, he holds a kylix—which was used for drinking water diluted wine.

The animalistic vitality of this composition is all the more remarkable when we consider that archaic compositions of only a few decades earlier were uncompromisingly stiff and unemotional.

Masterpieces of Greek Art

Caria, AR stater, ca. 420 BC

This intriguing depiction of a flying Nike seems to be a fine example of the artistic convention referred to as "archaizing". But Dr. Walker more appropriately sees it as "modernizing". The city of origin is uncertain, but running winged figures are not uncommon on early coins of Caria. The curved wings, twisted torso and rigid angular treatment of the extremities are stylistically archaic; but other features like hair style, profile eye and drapery are classical in style. Transparent drapery with sweeping folds is especially associated with late fifth century style in sculpture. This is not a transitional piece, but rather a deliberate rendering of the subject in the style of an earlier age—which to Greeks of the fifth century was venerable. Neither should it be considered a copy of an earlier work. The Carian celator has crafted here a wonderful modernized treatment of an old and popular subject, adding to it the advances of the Classical Period. Just as the city from which this piece was issued remains anonymous, so too does the artist who left his mark only in the timeless beauty of his work.

Masterpieces of Greek Art

Kamarina, Sicily, AR tetradrachm, ca. 420 BC

One version of this masterful depiction of Herakles, wearing the scalp of the Nemean Lion, has been attributed by Seltman to the engraver Exakestidas. He cited one die bearing the signature *Εξακεσ*, and saw similarities in style with another coin from Kamarina signed by this celator. The type is, of course, a precursor to the type employed in staggering numbers by Alexander the Great. The motif was not an invention of Exakestidas, but no other treatment of the motif works, in terms of balance and clarity, quite so well as this version from Kamarina. On many later imitations, it is difficult even to imagine the head of a lion in the confused headdress. The specimen illustrated here is slightly earlier than Seltman's specimen and reflects a more mature style. It differs in that Herakles is presented here wearing a full beard and moustache, as opposed to being clean shaven. It is impossible to say that this also is the work of Exakestidas, but it clearly is the work of a master engraver of equal ability.

Masterpieces of Greek Art

Katana, Sicily, AR tetradrachm, ca. 420 BC

This unsigned die is one of the most sensitive works emerging from Sicily at the height of its artistic greatness. Apollo is depicted here as a pensive young man—a much less idealized god than seen on its forerunners. The boyish hair style and long eyelashes, thin but faintly expressive lips, and smooth cameo-like skin combine to form an image of serenity and unworldly beauty. The leaf of wild parsley set in the field behind is actually the mark of the artist, appearing in lieu of a signature. Rizzo has been named this celator "The Master of the Leaf". Other specimens of this type, which are clearly from the same school, if not the same hand, bear bay leaves in this position. A nearly contemporary tetradrachm from Leontini (SNG ANS - 257), also of exceptional style and perhaps related, also bears a bay leaf in the field.

Masterpieces of Greek Art

Syracuse, AR tetradrachm, ca. 415 BC

The celator Kimon created this stunning depiction of the nymph Arethusa about 415 BC for the city of Syracuse in Sicily. According to Greek mythology, Arethusa was one of the Nereids, that is, one of the fifty daughters of Nereus and Doris. The Nereids were salt water nymphs as opposed to the spring nymphs of inland waters. One myth relates a story of the river god Alpheos (a river in the Peloponnesos) who pursued the nymph Arethusa. They both were changed to streams which flowed under the sea, surfacing finally in Ortygia, an island near Syracuse. Portrayals of Arethusa are common on the coinage of Syracuse, but none match the power and vitality of this extraordinary version. The beautiful and demure Arethusa seems to be suspended in water as the nymph's hair floats effortlessly in defiance of gravity with dolphins playing in the background. The signature of the artist rests proudly on the headband which lies framed by locks of billowing hair.

Masterpieces of Greek Art

Akragas, AR tetradrachm, ca. 415 BC

It has been suggested by Seltman that this composition is the work of Polykrates. The specimen illustrated here is undoubtedly by the same hand as that which engraved the dies for the Akragantine dekadrachm. Notwithstanding its smaller size, the tetradrachm is perhaps more appealing as a work of art because the field is not cluttered with the peculiar and obnoxious grasshopper that appears on the dekadrachm. The design is a remarkable creation, with one eagle about to devour its prey and the other screeching triumphantly. It seems to echo the words of Aeschylus which describe an omen witnessed by Agamemnon and Menelaus, in which two eagles (representing the two kings) devour a pregnant hare. The city ethnic is laid out in an ingenious way that does not interfere with the motif, and actually wraps back onto itself with the alpha serving as the first and final letters of the abbreviated ΑΚΡΑΓΑ [ΝΤΙΝΟΝ]. At a time when Sicilian cities vied for supremacy in the world of numismatic art, this composition must have left even seasoned connoisseurs in awe.

Masterpieces of Greek Art

Amphipolis, AR tetradrachm, ca. 410-354 BC

Amphipolis, on the eastern bank of the Strymon between Macedon and Thrace, was colonized by the Athenians in 437 BC. It was under their control for only a short time, as it fell to the Spartans in 424 and eventually to Philip II of Macedon in 357. Following liberation from Athens, the worship of Athena was abandoned and Apollo and Artemis were adopted as patrons of the city.

This head of Apollo, facing slightly to the right, is one of the great masterpieces of classical art. It combines power and serenity in a way that few artists were able. Seltman *(Masterpieces of Greek Coinage)*, noting stylistic similarities with Kimon's facing head of Arethusa from Syracuse, has suggested that he may also have created dies for Amphipolis. Although this is conjectural (dating is problematic), it may certainly be said that a celator of Kimon's ability must have been commissioned for the project. The subtle wreath of laurel, resting on long swept back hair, pushes forward just enough locks to create a sense of depth and to frame the expertly modelled face in this beautifully simple composition.

Masterpieces of Greek Art

Katana, AR tetradrachm, ca. 410 BC

This famous head of Apollo, by the master celator Herakleidas, ranks as one of the great works of Sicilian classical art. It is a vibrant composition for the period—avant-garde, one might say—and is an early example of the experimentation with baroque designs that marked the close of the fifth century. The unrestrained laurel wreath seems not to crown the god, but to become one with his wild flowing locks. It is difficult to envision whether the wreath becomes part of the hair or the hair becomes part of the wreath. High relief and strong lines in the face itself create a sensation of depth and intensity that counterbalances this fanciful hairstyle. The result is a work of tension and subtle complexity.

Unlike most signed dies, this one is boldly inscribed with the artist's full name, placed conspicuously in the obverse field. Only his great skill saves the piece from the taint of ostentation. In the perennial rivalry between Katana and Syracuse for artistic supremacy, this numismatic masterpiece must have fared well.

Masterpieces of Greek Art

Syracuse, Sicily, AR tetradrachm, ca. 410 BC

The signature of Eukleidas on this magnificent die leaves no question as to whom the credit belongs. The composition was undoubtedly inspired by the chryselephantine (gold and ivory) statue of Athena Parthenos at Athens, made by Pheidias some fifty years earlier . It is unlikely that even the great master of Parthenon fame could have surpassed the skill of Eukleidas in this technically perfect tribute. It is amazing how the artist was able to reach out and almost touch pretension without actually embracing it. Jenkins has reminded us that Athena was an important deity, and was honored with a temple at Syracuse (as in many other places). So, we should not be surprised to find her image on Syracusan coins, but rather that it is exceptional. Still, one can't help but sense a broader purpose in this effort. It almost seems to say "I, Eukleidas, am equal to the best!". Since we do not have the original work by Pheidias to answer the challenge we will never know. One thing we can say with certainty, however, Eukleidas was one of the greatest celators of his time, and his time was perhaps the greatest period in the entire history of art.

Masterpieces of Greek Art

Syracuse, Sicily, AR dekadrachm, ca. 405 BC

Following defeat of the Athenians in 413, Syracuse issued an impressive series of large silver coins in the denomination of ten drachms. These coins were struck over a period of approximately twenty years, with some dies being signed by the artists Kimon, Euainetos and Eukleidas. Besides being more anatomically correct than earlier representations, the technical problem of placing four horses abreast is solved here by turning the composition slightly toward the viewer. The chariot wheels are drafted in a three-quarter perspective that anchors the angle of view. This creates a dimensionality that is further enhanced by the ingenious placement of trophies in the foreground. Many inferior examples of this motif simply line up the trophies side by side, loosing that element of perspective.

The scene represents a quadriga race, at the point where the vehicle starts to round the turnpole. The head of the outside pole horse (third from right) is drawn back as the charioteer draws in the reins. Likewise, the inside trace horse lifts his head in anticipation of the crowding that will force a turn. The outside trace horse, farthest back in the composition, stretches in a full gallop—unaware of the impending move. Above, Nike crowns what will obviously be the victor.

Masterpieces of Greek Art

Syracuse, Sicily, AR tetradrachm, ca. 400 BC

The female head on this unsigned die from Syracuse has been attributed to an unknown master die engraver of the time or school of Eukleidas. It has been seen both as Arethusa, and as Nike. The latter interpretation stems from its association with the Syracusan coin depicting Athena (see earlier "Masterpiece" of 410 BC), which was designed by Eukleidas himself—and from the position of the head which appears to be flying.

The dolphins surrounding the head are a standard attribute of Arethusa on Syracusan coins, and their isolated appearance on the Athena type does not prove them to be a municipal badge or emblem of broader significance. The figure here may be seen as flying, or also as swimming. In either case, the earring and necklace hang naturally. The latter, and an interpretation of the subject as Arethusa, seems more fitting.

Stylistically, this image is very much like the youthful head of Apollo from Katana (see earlier "Masterpiece" of 420 BC). The application of artistic principles and engraver tendencies in these two pieces seems consistent. Both pieces are unsigned, but could be the work of a single artist.

Masterpieces of Greek Art

Syracuse, Sicily, AR dekadrachm, ca. 390 BC

The signed dekadrachms of Euainetos and Kimon are among the most prestigious coins in the Greek series. This specimen, signed along the lower edge of the coin by the celator Euainetos, is a beautiful example of classical Greek art at its best. The subject of this composition is Persephone, the daughter of Demeter who was abducted by Hades and became his wife—choosing to live half of her life in the nether world with her husband, and the other half with her mother and family on Earth. The dolphins around have traditionally been considered an attribute of Arethusa, but should more likely be treated in a broader sense as emblematic of the city Syracuse. These coins were very popular and highly regarded in their own time, even though they were probably not circulated extensively. A distinctive type of contemporary pottery includes the design which was made by impressing the coin into a mold. The coins themselves were sometimes set in silver dinnerware as a roundel. The dekadrachm (ten drachms) was a large and heavy silver coin of impressive substance. It has throughout time been the object of collector interest, even though it is not one of the rarer types in the Greek series.

Masterpieces of Greek Art

Pantikapaion, AV stater, ca. 350 BC

This vibrant representation of Pan, the god of flocks and shepherds portrays the awesome aspects of his divinity. Pan was dreaded by travellers because he often startled them and caused a sensation of terror and fear or "panic". This is in stark contrast to the pastoral scenes of Pan with reed flute and dancing fauns. In the former mode he was often appealed to by armies for aid in routing their enemies. As a representative symbol of the metropolis of Pantikapaion, the head of Pan appears on a number of coins from that city. None, however, match the emotion of this exceptional work. The fact that masterful Greek artists served patrons on the northern shores of the Black Sea is borne out not only by this piece, but by large finds of contemporary gold metalwork produced for Skythian kings. The richness of these finds would seem to indicate that cities of the Cimmerian Bosporos, and the surrounding area, were not only wealthy, but endowed with a sense of appreciation for fine art.

Masterpieces of Greek Art

Phalanna, Thessaly, AR drachm, ca. 340 BC

This unidentified male head is similar in style to the depiction of Apollo on gold staters and small bronze coins of Philip II of Macedon. It is one of many remarkable images engraved for minor coinage, and the workmanship actually surpasses that on many of the Macedonian staters. Sensitive modelling of the nose, lips and eye create a reflective pose that balances the loose and youthful hairstyle in a very sculptural motif. This tightly cropped image fairly jumps off the surface of the coin . Struck at the beginning of the Hellenistic Period, it embodies the best of what is yet to come in Hellenistic style.

Phalanna was a town of the Perrhaebi, a powerful warlike people of northern Thessaly, located on the banks of the Peneus river. The district known as Perrhaebia bordered on Macedon. It is very possible that the image on this coin and that on the coins of Philip of Macedon are related. It seems likely that those struck for Philip would retain a more conservative style while the artist employed at Phalanna might be given a free reign to create something more avantgarde. The omission of Apollo's laurel wreath may have been a purposeful device to avoid any appearance of subservience to Philip. It is conceivable that the same artist produced designs for Philip and Phalanna.

Masterpieces of Greek Art

Metapontum, Italy, AR nomos, ca. 330 BC

Leukippos was the legendary founder of Metapontum, but precisely which figure in mythology this might be is uncertain. Among the series of silver coins struck at that city is a double stater (nomos) bearing the hero's likeness. One of the most talented artists working at Metapontum signed his dies with the letters AMI... which are included in the reverse design of this coin [see AMI in the section on signed dies]. We can assume that this is a signature because another die of identical style, but variant treatment of decoration, is signed AMI... on both obverse and reverse. This parallel die (Jenkins *Ancient Greek Coins* #318) also bears a magistrate's name—eliminating that probability for the shortened inscription.

The execution of this die is a tour de force of late classical style. The modelling of facial features is exceptionally delicate, yet it retains that feeling of strength required of the subject. The impressive beard is dominant without being ostentatious, and the curls of hair peeking out from below a beautifully simple helmet are punctuated by tiny wisps along the neck—an unusual and effective device. A tiny lion's head in the field is obviously an accommodation to mint bureaucracy. The overall balance of composition and skill in the hand of the engraver marks this work as an unqualified masterpiece.

Masterpieces of Greek Art

Alexander III, Arados, AR tetradrachm, ca. 328-320 BC

An Alexander tetradrachm may not seem a likely candidate for a "Masterpiece of Greek Art". The motif was so standardized that it really was not necessary to hire a master engraver to produce dies for this issue, especially not for reverse dies. Nonetheless, Arados did just that. The (by this time) standard depiction of Zeus was probably inspired by the chryselephantine statue of Zeus at Olympia created by Pheidias more than a century earlier. The anatomy on this version follows the canon of Polykleitos even though the work of Lysippos was well known by the time this coin was struck. Of particular note is excellent detail in the face, hands and feet. These elements pose great difficulty for the average engraver. Also notable is the adept foreshortening of the left leg, which gives the viewer a 3/4 facing perspective. The high-backed throne, although simple, is also designed with much greater care than typical examples of the same motif. Even the inscription is rendered with greater precision and balance than typically found on these issues. The net result is a work of superior appeal and timeless beauty, the more so because contemporary specimens of this motif normally are not.

Masterpieces of Greek Art

Sicily, AR tetradrachm, ca. 320 BC

The most notable coinage of North Africa is that produced by the Carthaginians during their occupation of Sicily. Bearing the Punic inscription "People of the Camp", the issues struck by Hamilkar and his invasion force are as artistically appealing as any of the contemporary local issues. This is due, no doubt, to the Carthaginian employment of Sicilian die engravers. While Sicilian in style and fabric, the images on these issues are typically North African. This makes for a wonderfully artistic series. The impressive tetradrachm presented here features a female head with necklace, wearing a Phrygian felt cap that is bound with an embroidered ribbon decorated with palmette-like flora. Falling from beneath the ties of the cap are twisted ringlets of long hair, styled in Punic fashion. The subject was formerly regarded as Dido, the mythical founder of Carthage, but is now thought to be Artemis-Tanit or a variant.

Masterpieces of Greek Art

Pyrrhos, Epeiros, AR tetradrachm, ca. 295-272 BC

Pyrrhos was an intrepid military adventurer who shows up at the unlikeliest of places. From Ipsos, to Syracuse and Macedon to Sparta, he marched a tattered army into impossible situations and all but once managed to survive. See the section on Syracuse for more about his interesting life. This tetradrachm was produced at Lokroi Epizephyrioi in Italy where Pyrrhos was on campaign against the Romans.

This bearded head of Zeus Dodonaios is executed in typical Hellenistic fashion, full of vitality and explosive virtuosity. The traditional laurel wreath is replaced by one of oak, which is an allusion to the sacred oaks of Dodona in Epeiros. The oracle at this place was dedicated to Zeus, and the will of the god was indicated by wind rustling through the sacred trees. In order to read the messages more easily, bells and noise makers were tied to the upper branches.

Masterpieces of Greek Art

Terina, Bruttium, AR drachm, ca. 300 BC

This design of Nike seated on a cippos (small altar) and holding a bird in her right hand is derived from an earlier work by the master celator Phrygillos, who worked at Terina about 425 BC. The prototype is rather pensive, whereas this composition reveals an inquisitive and alert goddess—more appropriate as a representation of victory. While the work of Phrygillos is masterful, beyond dispute, this treatment succeeds on its own merits. Considering that this is a tiny coin of only 2.6 grams, the detail, especially in Nike's wings and drapery, is exceptional. This motif improves on the earlier version in that the ethnic TEPINAIΩN is moved from the reverse to the obverse. This allows a clean field for displaying what is clearly the preferred image. Subtleties like the turned ankle, distribution of weight, and lithe flow of the anatomy mark this as a work turning the corner from Classicism to Hellenism.

Masterpieces of Greek Art

Syracuse, Sicily, AR 16 litra, ca. 214-212 BC

    This bold portrait of Zeus is an extraordinary example of the fully developed Hellenistic style. Following the murder of Hieron's grandson, Hieronymos, a new democracy was established at Syracuse and Zeus was honored as the patron and protector of the city. As a result, the portraits of Hieron and his family were replaced with representations of deities. This coinage lasted only two years as Syracuse fell to the Romans in 212. The idealized god of earlier generations gives way here to a very humanized portrayal—easily enough mistaken for a king or hero. A protruding brow, raised bridge, fleshiness about the eyes and full lips all add to the character of the subject as an individual. Although the features are those of a mortal, this treatment still conveys a feeling of power and stature that becomes a god.

Masterpieces of Greek Art

Eukratides, Baktria, AR tetradrachm, ca. 170-145 BC

Eukratides attained power through revolt, and became the uncontested King of Baktria following his elimination of Demetrios II. His reign was one of peace through power, but ended in assassination by the hand of his own son, Heliokles. In the entire series of Baktrian coinage, which is replete with the images of major and minor kings, no better example of Hellenistic portraiture exists than that of Eukratides on this magnificent tetradrachm. Engraved by a master celator, the strength and character of this enigmatic leader are expertly captured in a powerfully emotional pose. It must rank, with the contemporary portrait coin of Orophernes from Cappadocia, as one of the most successful efforts of the Hellenistic age. It is interesting, if not surprising, that these two masterpieces originate in the East. The great sculptors of antiquity are usually thought of in connection with Athens, Sicily or the Greek islands. Whether Eukratides and Orophernes imported talent for the occasion, or peerless engravers emerged locally, is unknown.

Masterpieces of Greek Art

Orophernes, Cappadocia, AR tetradrachm, ca. 158-156 BC

Orophernes, a supposed (illegitimate) son of Ariarathes IV, was sent off to Ionia to be raised after a legitimate heir was born. He was later brought back to Cappadocia, in opposition to Ariarathes V, by the Seleukid monarch Demetrios Soter. The reign, or usurpation, of Orophernes was short-lived as Attalos of Pergamon and his Roman allies helped to reinstate Ariarathes V. Although two obverse dies and six reverse dies are known, the surviving coins of Orophernes are extremely rare. With one possible exception, they have all come from a temple deposit at Priene discovered in 1870. Of the nine known specimens, not more than three are in private collections. While this coin is of the utmost historical importance, it is also a superb example of Hellenistic portraiture and a masterpiece of die engraving. In spite of a long tradition of portraiture in Cappadocia, nothing before or after this issue boasts greater sensitivity or technical merit. Is it possible, given that Orophernes was raised in Ionia, and upon his accession deposited an emergency treasury of some 400 talents at Priene, that the dies for this coinage were commissioned there?

Appendix

I   Glossary
II   Table of Events
III   Additional References
IV   Index

Appendix I — Glossary

The glossary in Volume I of *Ancient Coin Collecting* contains common terms that the collector of ancient coins will encounter. Following are some of the art historical terms and additional terms unique to Greek coinage that the reader and collector may find useful.

"After": A term that identifies a work as being deliberately copied from an original by another artist.
Amphora: A large two-handled vessel used to store or ship wine.
Avant-garde: Experimental or unconventional art for its time.
Chelys: Musical instrument, a form of lyre.
Chiton: A linen tunic, long or short, worn by men or women.
Chryselephantine: Combining gold with ivory.
Contrapposto: A twisting of the human form in which the head and shoulders face in a different direction than the hips and legs.
Daric: Gold coin of the Persians, possibly named after King Darios.
Debasement: Reduction in the precious metal content of a coin by adding an inferior metal to form an alloy.
Dekadrachm: Coin of ten drachms in value.
Diadochi: Successors, usually of Alexander the Great.
Didrachm, Diobol, etc.: Coin of two stated units in value.
Dodekadrachm: Coin of 12 drachms in value.
Drachm: The standard unit of weight against which other denominations are measured.
Epiphanes: God manifest.
Ethnic: The inscribed name of a city or of the people who issued a coin.
Euergetes: Benefactor.
Form: The presentation of shape rather than line to cause a perception.
Glyptic: Carved, as opposed to molded or modelled.
Hemidrachm, hemiobol, etc.: Coin of one-half stated unit in value.
Heraion: A temple of Hera.
Herm: A pillar, usually with a head mounted on top.
Hierax: Hawk.
Himation: A woolen mantle.
Keraunos: Thunderbolt.
Kore: A maiden, plural = Korai
Kylix: A wide shallow Greek drinking cup with two handles.
Kyrbasia: Headdress with ear flaps worn by Persian Satraps.
Lagobolon: Shepherd's staff, attribute of Pan.
Mamertini: Oscan mercenaries from Campania in Italy, who took their name from Mamers (Mars) and served other lands as mercenaries.
Modelling: The shaping of a workable substance.

Motif: A thematic element in a work of art.
Medium: Specific type of artistic technique or means of expression.
Narrative: A composition whose main purpose is to tell a story.
Nike: The goddess of victory, usually—but not always—winged.
Nikator: Victorious.
Nomos: Silver denomination equal to one stater, meaning "legal".
Octodrachm, Octobol, etc.: Coin of eight stated units in value.
Onkia: 1/12 of a Sicilian bronze litra.
Overstrike: Striking a new image over a previously struck coin.
Pegasi: Coins of Corinth and her colonies depicting Pegasos.
Pentadrachm, Pentobol, etc.: Coin of five stated units in value.
Pileus: Conical felt cap of the Dioscouri.
Plastic: Something molded or modelled, opposite of Glyptic.
Polos: Cylindrical headdress, often worn by Hera.
Philopator: Lover of one's father.
Relief: The degree to which a design projects from or sinks into the surface—normally expressed as deep/high or shallow/low.
Sandan: Deity of Tarsos in Cilicia, akin to Herakles.
Rhyton: A ceremonial drinking cup made in the shape of an animal's head—originally of eastern origin.
Sappho: Lyric poet of the late seventh century.
Satrap: Provincial governor in the Persian empire.
Shekel: Unit of coinage in Phoenicia, Judaea, etc.
Siglos: Standard silver coin of the Persians.
Soter: Savior.
Sphinx: Mythical monster with the head of a woman, and a lion's body.
Stephanophoros: Wreath-bearer.
Strategos: Military commander.
Tetradrachm, tetrobol, etc.: Coin of four stated units in value.
Tetrapolis; Pentapolis, etc.: a group of four cities; five cities, etc.
Theos: God.
Tiara: Oriental cap with three flaps.
Tyche: Goddess of fortune.
Wappenmünzen: Modern name given to heraldic coins from Athens.

Appendix II — Table of Events

ca. 620	—First coins struck in Lydia or Ionia
612	—Fall of Nineveh
587	—Capture of Jerusalem by Nebuchadnezzar
ca. 550	—First coins struck in Athens and Aigina
546	—Persian conquest of the kingdom of Croesus
480	—Xerxes invades Greece with 180,000 troops
479	—Greeks defeat the Persians at Plataea
456	—Temple of Zeus at Olympia completed; death of Aeschylus two years after writing the *Oresteia*.
447	—Building of the Parthenon
431	—Start of the second Peloponnesian War
362	—Thebes defeats Sparta at Mantinea
353	—Death of Maussollos, building of the Mausoleum
348	—Death of Plato
336	—Philip II murdered at Aigai, accession of Alexander the Great
334	—Alexander crosses into Asia Minor
331	—Alexander takes Babylon and Susa
330	—Alexander conquers Baktria and Sogdiana
323	—Death of Alexander the Great at Babylon
317	—Olympias, Alexander's mother, has Philip III assassinated, leaving Alexander's son sole monarch
309	—Murder of Alexander's son by Cassander
306	—Demetrios Poliorketes defeats Ptolemy in naval battle at Salamis in Cyprus
218	—Start of the Second Punic War
197	—Philip V defeated by Flamininus at Kynoskephalai
168	—Roman victory at Pydna ends Macedonian Kingdom
90	—Indo-Skythian invasion of Baktria
88	—Mithradatic War, massacre of Romans in Asia Minor
63	—Defeat of Mithradates by Pompey
30	—Cleopatra commits suicide at Alexandria

Appendix III — Additional References

The works listed here are mentioned in addition to those offered at the end of each section. Although they may not directly pertain to a specific subject covered in the text, they are included because they are useful to the collector who wishes to examine Greek coins as works of art. General attribution guides and published collections of Greek coins are listed in the bibliography to Volume I of *Ancient Coin Collecting*.

Agard, Walter R. *Classical Myths in Sculpture*, University of Wisconsin Press, 1951.
Akurgal, Ekrem. *Ancient Civilizations and Ruins of Turkey*, Istanbul, 1978.
Baldwin, Agnes. *Facing Heads on Ancient Greek Coins*, New York, 1914 (reprint 1982.
Bieber, Margarete. *Alexander the Great in Greek and Roman Art*, Chicago, 1964.
BMC —The *Catalogue of Greek Coins* in the British Museum is a 29 volume set of inestimable value to the student of this series.
Boardman, John. *Greek Art*, London, 1985.
Casson, Lionel and Martin Price. *Coins, Culture and History in the Ancient World*. Detroit, 1981.
Ehresmann, Julia M. *The Pocket Dictionary of Art Terms*, Boston, 1979.
Frey, Albert R. and Mark M. Salton. *Dictionary of Numismatic Names*, with *Glossary of Numismatic Terms in English, French, German, Italian and Swedish*, London, 1973.
Grace, Virginia. *Stamped Amphora Handles Found in the Athenian Agora, 1931-1932*, Athens, 1934.
Hill, G.F. *A Handbook of Greek and Roman Coins*, London, 1899.
Korshak, Yvonne. *Frontal Faces in Attic Vase Painting of the Archaic Period*, Chicago, 1987.
Lloyd, Seton. *A Traveller's History of Anatolia*, University of California Press, 1989.
Markman, Sidney D. *The Horse in Greek Art*, New York, 1969.
Osborne, Robin. *Classical Landscape with Figures*, London, 1987.
Renault, Mary. *The Nature of Alexander*, New York, 1975.
Richter, G.M.A. *A Handbook of Greek Art*, London, 1959.
_____. *Engraved Gems of the Greeks and the Etruscans, A History of Greek Art in Miniature*, London, 1968.
Scullard, H.H. *The Elephant in The Greek and Roman World*, Cornell University Press, 1974.
Stierlin, Henri. *The Cultural History of Greece*, Tr. Erika Abrams, Geneva, 1983.

General Index

A

Abdera 29
Achaean League 38
Achaios 136
Achilles 98
Aegean islands 40
Aegis 86
Aeschylus 26, 58, 101, 168
Agamemnon 47, 168
Agathokleia 150
Agathokles 26, 148
Agon 105
Aigai, Aiolis 62
Aigina 44
Aiolians 65
Aiolis 62
Aitna 26, 163
Aitna Master 163
Aitolian League 36, 38
Ajax "the lesser" 78, 98, 99
Akanthos 29
Akarnania 38
Akragas 84, 85, 168
Alexander I 31
Alexander I, Balas 138
Alexander II, Zebina 140
Alexander III 31, 33, 124, 178
Alexandria 61
Alpheos river 107, 167
Amastris 56, 127
Amazonomachy 63
Ambracia 36
Amphiktyones 38
Amphipolis 169
ampyx 92
Amyntas 153
Anaxilaos 26, 108
anchor 56
ancient literature 1
Andros 29, 32, 42, 113

Anthela 38
Antialkidas 151
Antigonid Dynasty 31
Antigonos Doson 32
Antigonos Gonatas 27, 32, 125
Antigonos Monopthalmos 125
Antimachos I 148
Antiochos I 97, 135
Antiochos II 135
Antiochos III 50, 136
Antiochos IV 137
Antiochos IX 140
Antiochos V 137
Antiochos VI 139
Antiochos VII 139
Antiochos VIII 140
Antiochos X 141
Antiochos XI 141
Antiochos XII 142
Antiochos XIII 142
Antiphellos 121
Apelles 34, 49
Aphrodite 53, 61, 93
Apollo 32, 36, 38, 56, 62, 63, 77, 107, 113, 166, 169, 170, 173, 176
Apollo Delphinios 37
Apollo Grynios 63
Apollodotos 99
Apollodotos II 155
Apollonia Pontika 56, 59
Apollophanes 156
Aptera 85
Arados 70, 178
Arcadia 84, 85
Archaic Period 111
archaizing 16, 17
Archebios 154
Archelaos 134
Archilochos 50
Arethusa 83, 92, 161, 167, 173

Argonauts 58
Argos 47, 124
Ariadne 49
Ariaramnes 131
Ariarathes III 131
Ariarathes IV 131
Ariarathes IX 133
Ariarathes V 131
Ariarathes VI 132
Ariarathes VII 132
Ariarathes VIII 132
Ariarathes X 134
Ariobarzanes I 133
Ariobarzanes II 133
Ariobarzanes III 133
Aristotle 124
Arkadian League 39
Arsinoe I 143
Arsinoe II 143
Arsinoe III 144
Artaxerxes 64
Artemidoros 154
Artemis 60, 72, 91, 169, 179
Artemis Leucophryene 64
Asia Minor 60, 62
Askalon 146
Asklepios 49, 130, 162
Asopos 44
Aspendos 89, 99, 106
Asterion 103
Athena 33, 41, 46, 63, 98, 171
Athens 41, 42, 46
Athletic Events 105
Atlas 46
Attalos II 130

B

Baal 33, 34
Babylon 33
Baktrian Kings 147
Baktria 72, 183
Barka, Hamilkar 21
Barke 72

baroque 77
Battle of Mycale 50
Battle of Plataea 74
Berenike I 143
Berenike II 144
Bisalti 30
Black Sea Area 56, 57, 58
Black Sea Hoard 59
Bodashtart 70
Boeotarchs 39
Boeotian League 39
Bosporos 56
Brettian League 39

C

Caria 164
Carthage 26, 27, 39, 72, 161
Cassius 133
Cayster river 60
celature 74
Chaeronea 38
Chalkidian League 39
Chalkis 39
Chares of Lindos 50, 78
Chios 30, 49, 101
Choirion 78, 85
chronology 16
Cimmerian Bosporos 56, 175
Cimmerian invasion 57, 64
cippos 181
Cleopatra I 145
Cleopatra II 145
Cleopatra III 146
Cleopatra Selene 146
Cleopatra Thea 140
Cleopatra VII 146
coin motifs 94
Colossus of Rhodes 78
Corinth 46, 105
counterfeits 59
countermarks 9
Crete 52
Croesus 3, 4, 12, 60

191

Cumae 22, 90
Curetes 52
Cyclades 49, 50
Cyprus 53

D

Daidalos 52
Daidalos of Sicyon 81
Damastion 30
Danube 90
Dating 13
dating 13, 16
Delos 50
Delphi 37, 38, 74, 89, 95, 100, 105
Demarete 161
Demareteion 43, 117, 161
Demareteion Master 81, 161
Demeter 38, 57, 174
Demetrios I 147
Demetrios I, 138
Demetrios II 139
Demetrios II, Baktria 149
Demetrios III 141
Demetrios III, Aniketos 152
Demetrios Poliorketes 27, 31, 32, 50, 53, 125
denominations 4, 11, 12, 60
Derrones 30, 76
Dido 179
die studies 15
dies 7, 8, 75
Diodotos I 147
Diodotos II 147
Diomedes 152
Dione 46
Dionysios, Baktria 156
Dionysios I, Syracuse 78
Dionysios the Elder 157
Dionysos 25, 29, 30, 49, 51, 61, 86, 160, 163
Dioscouri 90
Dioskourias 58
diskobolos 107

Dodona 180
dolphin 49
Dorian Pentapolis 107
Dorians 44, 50, 60
Doris 167

E

Ebusus 21
Edones 30
electrum 4
Elis 46
Endymion 63
engraved gems 79
Epander 153
Epeiros 36, 38, 180
Ephesos 60, 70
Epidauros 44
Eretria 40, 113
Etenna 106
Euainetos 79, 81, 172, 174
Euarchidas 82
Euboian league 40
Eukleidas 82, 171, 172, 173
Eukratides 149, 183
Eukratides II 149
Eumenes II 126
Eumenos 80, 82
Europa 52, 103
Eurymedon 43, 53
Euthydemos I 147
Euthydemos II 148
Euthymos 80, 82
Euxine 57
Exakestidas 82, 165
Exekias 96

F

facing heads 75
Flamininus, T. Quinctius 126

G

Gaul 21
Gela 26

Gelon 157, 161
gems 96
Glykon 97
Golden Fleece 58
gorgon 75
Gortyna 104
Greek culture 18, 19

H

Hannibal 39
Hasdrubal 21
Heliodoros 137
Heliokles and Laodike 149
Heliokles I 150
Heliokles II 151
Helios 50
Hellenistic Period 119
Hera 56
Hera Hoplosmia 39
Herakleia 22, 83, 84
Herakleia ad Latmon 63
Herakleidas 78, 170
Herakles 33, 72, 95, 127
Hermaios 155
Hermogenes 64
Herodotus 43, 74
Hesiod 101
Hierax 123, 135, 136
Hieron 26
Hieron II 123, 157
Hieronymos 157
Himera 84
Hippodamia 46
Hippostratos 155
Homer 51, 65, 101
hoplite race 108
Hydaspes 34
Hyele 84
Hypsas 162

I

Ichnai 30
Illyro-Paeonian region 30

incuse designs 114
inscriptions 19
Ionia 60, 62
Ionians 65
Ipsos 180
Isthmian games 47, 105
Istros 90
Itanos 52

J

Jason 58
Juba II 146

K

Kabeiros 21
Kalliope 155
Kalymna 113
Kamarina 82, 83, 165
Kassandra 98, 99
Katana 26, 77, 81, 85, 166, 170
Kaulonia 22, 159
kausia 34
Kelenderis 107
Keos 49
Kherei 121
Kimon 37, 83, 117, 167, 172, 174
Kition 53
Klazomenai 80, 85, 89
Knossos 52, 102
Kolchis 58, 63
korymbos 92
Kos 49
Krateros 127
Kromna 56
Kroton 22, 114
Kybele 65
Kydnos 61
Kydonia 80, 84
Kyme 61, 63
Kynoskephalai 32, 125, 126
Kyrene 72
Kyzikos 93, 107, 108, 111, 121, 160

193

L

Labors of Herakles 97
Labyrinth 52
Lagids 143
Laiai 30
Laios 100
Lampsakos 61
Laodike, (Wife and sister
 of Demetrios) 138
Laodike, (wife of
 Mithradates IV) 128
Laos 89, 115
Larissa 37, 40
Laurion mines 43
leagues 19, 38
Leontini 77, 81, 84, 89
Leptines 157
Lesbos 90
Leukas 36
Leukippos 177
Lion's Scalp 86
Lion's Scalp 95
Lokroi Epizephyrioi 180
Lokroi Opontii 78
Lycian League 40
Lydia 3, 60
Lysias 151
Lysippos 48, 78, 119, 178
Lyttos 52

M

Macedon 125, 180
Maeander 60, 64
Magas of Kyrene 144
magistrates 14
Magna Graecia 22, 114
Magnesia 50, 64, 136
Mallos 96
Mamertini 26
Mannerism 77
Map, Peloponnesos 46
Map, Sicily 25

marble 50
Mardonius 51
Mark Antony 134
Maroneia 30
Massalia 81, 83, 85
Master of the Leaf 166
Mauretania 146
Media 138
Melos 89
Melqarth 72
Menander II, Dikaios 154
Menander, Soter 150
Mende 29
Menelaus 168
mercenaries 19, 26
Mesembria 59
Messana 26, 81, 108
Metapontum 81, 85, 115, 177
mines 6, 51
Minos 52, 103
Minotaur 52, 102
Mint Cities 21, 24, 28, 35, 45, 48,
 54, 55, 58, 66, 67,
 68, 71, 73
mints 44
Mithradates III 128
Mithradates IV 128
Mithradates V 128
Mithradates VI 129, 132
Mithrapata 121
Mithridates VI 58
monetary standards 8, 10
Mostis 126
Mycenaeans 50, 60, 95
Myron 84, 96
Mythology 94

N

narrative 111
Naxos, Cyclades 49
Naxos, Sicily 25, 85, 163
Nemea 95, 105
Nemean Lion 95, 97, 165

Nereus 167
Nestus river 29
Nike 33, 34, 76, 164, 172, 173, 181
Nike of Samothrace 53
Nikias 154
Nikomedes I 129
Nikomedes II 130
Nikomedes III 130
Nikomedes IV 130
Numismatic art 74
Nysa 132

O

Odysseos 98
Oedipus 37, 49, 100, 101
Oenomalis 46
Oileus 98
Olbia 57
Olympia 81, 105, 178
Olympic Games 47
Olympic games 81
Olympios 79
Olympus 31
Olynthos 39
Orophernes 184
Orreskioi 30
Ortygia 167

P

Paeonia 30
Palladium 98
Pan 32, 56, 175
Pan-Hellenic games 105, 106
Pandosia 115
Panormos 27
Pantaleon 148
Pantikapaion 56, 175
Paphos 53
Paros 50
Parthenon 41, 117, 161
Patraos 122
Pausanius 1

Peace of Apamea 50
Pegasos 46
Peisistratus 41
Peloponnesian War 41, 44, 46
Peloponnesos 38, 46
Pergamon 61
Perikle 121
Perikles 41
Periods of Greek Art 109
Perrhaebi 176
Persephone 160, 174
Perseus 122, 125, 138
Persian War 41, 44, 51, 74
Peukolaos 153
Phaistos 104
Phalanna 176
Phalasarna 52
Pharnabazos 121
Pharnakes I 128
Phayllos 107
Pheidias 41, 161, 171, 178
Philetairos 126
Philetas 49
Philip II 31, 38, 39, 99, 105, 122, 169, 176
Philip, Philadelphos 142
Philip V 32, 122, 125
Philistis 157
Philoxenos 152
Phoenicia 70, 104
Phokaia 89
Phrygia 46
Phrygillos 79, 84, 96, 181
Pindar 58
Plataea 31, 43
Plato 74
Plato, Baktria 150
Pliny 1, 34
Plutarch 34
Pnytagoras 53
Polybos 100
Polykleitos 78, 81
Polykrates 85, 168
Polyrhenion 85

195

Polyxenos 152
pomegranate 61
Pompey the Great 129, 142
Pontic Kingdom 58
Poros 34
portraiture 120
Poseidon 32, 41, 98
Poseidon Hippios 112
Poseidonia 116
Potidaia 112
pottery 41, 47, 63, 74, 75, 76, 96, 111, 112
Priam 98
Priapos 61
Priene 132, 184
production of coinage 6
Prokles 85
Protogoras 29
Prusias I 129
Prusias II 130
Ptolemy I 31, 143
Ptolemy II 143
Ptolemy III 144
Ptolemy IV 144
Ptolemy V 122, 145
Ptolemy VI 145
Ptolemy VIII 145
Ptolemy XII 146
Pumiathon 53
pun 86, 89, 113
Punic Wars 72
Purchasing power 4
Pylaimenes 127
Pyrrhos 22, 27, 36, 180
Pythagoras 50
Pythian games 37, 38, 105

R

ram horns 86
Rhadamanthus 103
Rhegion 83
Rhegion, Bruttium 23
Rhodos 50, 89

rhyta 74
Romans 26, 27
Roxana 34

S

saccos 93
Salamis 44, 51
Salamis, Cyprus 31, 53
Samos 50
Sappho 36
Sardeis 65, 136
Saronic Gulf 44, 51
Sarpedon 52, 103
Segesta 92
Seleukid Dynasty 135
Seleukos I 122, 135
Seleukos II 135
Seleukos III 136
Seleukos IV 137
Seleukos VI 141
Selge 106
Selinus 113, 162
Seneca 101
Shekel of Tyre 70
Sibyl 22
Sicily 25, 72
Siculo-Punic 72, 179
Sicyon 48
Side 61
Sidon 70
signatures 80, 81, 112, 167, 170, 171, 172, 177
Silenus 163
Silphium 72
Simonides 49
Sinope 57
Skarphea 99
Skythia 63
Skythians 56, 175
Smyrna 65
Sogdiana 34
Sophocles 101
Sosion 85

Sparta 37, 46, 180
sphendone 93
Sphinx 49, 100
stephane 64
Stephanophoroi 62
Strato I 150
Strato II 156
Stratonike 131
Strymon River 39
Strymon river 30, 31
style 76, 77, 111, 119
Sybaris 116
Syracuse 81, 82, 84, 85, 161, 167, 171, 172, 173, 180

T

Tagus 40
Tanit 72, 179
Taras 23, 81, 83, 116
Tarsos 61, 96
Tauric Chersonese 56
Temenids 31, 124
Temenus 31, 124
Tenedos 51
Terina 84, 181
Thasos 51
Thebes 37, 100
Themistokles 43, 64
Theocritus 101
Theodotos 85
Theophilos 153
Theopompus 101
Thermai 83
Theseus 49, 102
Thessalian League 40
Thourioi 82, 83, 84
Thucydides 46
Timarchos 138
Tissaphernes 121
tondo 75, 96
trade 18
Trapezos 89
Triopian games 107

Troas 51
Trojan War 98
Tryphon 139
turtle 44
Tyche 70
Tyre 70

V

Velia 82, 83, 84, 112

W

Wappenmünzen 42
wrestling 106

X

Xanthos 121
Xenophon 119
Xerxes 31, 44

Z

Zaielioi 30
Zankle 89
Zeugitana 72
Zeus 33, 34, 46, 56, 61, 103, 104, 178
Zeus Dodonaios 180
Zoilos I 151